Lernthriller Englisch

W0110241

BONE BY BONE

Gina Billy

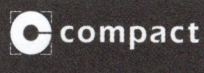

compact

Weitere Informationen zu Compact Lernthrillern finden Sie am Ende des Buches und unter www.lernkrimi.de.

© Compact Verlag GmbH
Baierbrunner Straße 27, 81379 München
Ausgabe 2014

Chefredaktion: Dr. Matthias Feldbaum
Redaktion: Helga Aichele
Fachkorrektur: Nathalie Russell
Produktion: Ute Hausleiter
Titelabbildung: fotolia.com, katalinks
Lernkrimi-Logo: Carsten Abelbeck
Gestaltung: EKH Werbeagentur München GbR, textum GmbH
Umschlaggestaltung: EKH Werbeagentur München GbR, Hartmut Baier

ISBN 978-3-8174-9497-2
381749497/1

www.compactverlag.de, www.lernkrimi.de

VORWORT

Liebe Leserin, lieber Leser,

mitreißend und unheimlich spannend – die Compact Lernthriller mit ihrer Kombination aus fesselnder Lektüre und didaktischem Übungsanteil eignen sich hervorragend, um breite Sprachkompetenzen in der Fremdsprache zu erwerben. Der Lerner wird dabei durch die atemberaubende Handlung, das angemessene Sprachniveau und den stetig ansteigenden Schwierigkeitsgrad der Übungen gefördert und motiviert. Ein ausführlicher Abschlusstest ermöglicht das Wiederholen und Festigen des Gelernten. In einem alphabetischen Glossar am Ende des Buches sind noch einmal übersichtlich alle Vokabeln zum Nachschlagen aufgelistet.

So lernen Sie mit Compact Lernlektüren:
• **Mit Begeisterung lernen:** Die packende Handlung motiviert Sie beim Lesen des englischen Originaltextes.
• **Wissen intensivieren und erweitern:** Durch die Kombination aus didaktisierter Lektüre und textbezogenen Übungen testen und trainieren Sie Ihre Sprachkenntnisse effektiv. Vokabelangaben auf jeder Seite unterstützen Sie beim Lesen.
• **Systematisch lernen:** Knüpfen Sie an Ihr individuelles Sprachniveau an und setzen Sie eigene Lernziele – linear im Schwierigkeitsgrad ansteigend oder mit punktuellen Schwerpunkten von Grundwortschatz bis Hörverstehen.
• **Unabhängig sein:** Lernen Sie ganz individuell – wo und wann Sie wollen.

Viel Spaß beim **spannend Englisch lernen**
wünscht Ihnen

Prof. Dr. Christiane Neveling
Didaktik der romanischen Sprachen, Universität Leipzig

3

INHALT

ZU DIESEM BUCH

Mit dem brutalen Axtmord an einem Politiker beginnt für die Londoner Polizei und den Profiler Clay Sheridan ein Wettlauf gegen die Zeit. Denn der Killer verwickelt die Ermittler in ein perfides Katz-und-Maus-Spiel, während er Mord für Mord einen blutigen Rachefeldzug führt.

Als Knochen der Opfer in Yorkshire auftauchen, wächst die Vermutung, dass die Morde mit einem lange zurückliegenden Skandal zusammenhängen. Clay und die Ermittler versuchen fieberhaft, den Killer zu stoppen, doch der hat schon das nächste Opfer in seiner Gewalt ...

1 CHILLED TO THE BONE

Estelle Ashworth takes another little **sip** of her vodka tonic. It's strong – just the way she likes it. She tells herself not to drink too much – not yet. She must **keep up appearances**. Her eyes move around the room of her home in London's exclusive Belgravia neighbourhood.

Candles and flowers are everywhere in the large, elegant room. It takes up most of the first floor, which is unusual for a town-house. The room is perfect for **entertaining**. It has a small bar and several comfortable chairs and sofas. A musician is playing quiet, background music on the black **grand piano**. Only a few guests are left at the party.

sip	Schlückchen
to keep up appearances	den Anschein wahren
entertaining	*hier*: Gäste bewirten
grand piano	Flügel
entire	ganz
to outdo oneself	sich selbst übertreffen

Oh, I'm so glad it is almost over, Estelle thinks. Soon I can go upstairs and take off these party clothes. Then I'll have just one more drink, she promises herself. Thinking about being alone in her room makes Estelle smile. It's the first real one on her face the **entire** evening. For a moment, it makes Estelle look softer and younger than her 62 years. Then the smile is gone. Sarah Mead is coming over to say goodbye.

"Estelle, you have really **outdone yourself** tonight. This party for Malcolm's 60th birthday was just beautiful – one of your best

5

MP (Member of Parliament)	Parlamentsab-geordneter (GB)
to whisper	flüstern
pity	Mitleid
to give one's best to sb.	jmd. (liebe) Grüße ausrichten
It's a pity...	Schade, dass...
company	*hier*: Gesellschaft
expected	erwartet
the old days	früher, in alten Zeiten
fault	Schuld, Fehler
responsible	verantwortlich

ever. Malcolm is so lucky to have you as his wife."

"Thank you, Sarah. But I'm the lucky one," Estelle tells her.

Both women know that Estelle doesn't mean that. She's just being polite and is saying what a politician's wife should. Estelle is good at this kind of small talk. She's had years of practice, after all.

Across the room, she sees her husband, MP Malcolm Ashworth. He's laughing and helping a young woman put on her coat.

"Malcolm is also looking well and happy – and much younger than his age," Sarah adds. "Is that his new, um, assistant?"

"Yes. Ms Lisa Giles. Malcolm says she's very good at her job and a great help to him."

"I'm sure she is," Sarah says a little sarcastically.

The two of them see Lisa Giles whisper something to Malcolm before she finally goes out of the front door. Sarah looks at Estelle with pity in her eyes. Sarah and her husband, Landon, have known Estelle and Malcolm for over 40 years.

Malcolm will never change, Sarah thinks. But normally he's more discreet. It's clear that Estelle doesn't want to talk about it, though.

"Well, Estelle, I must be going, too. Thank you again for the lovely evening, and let's meet for lunch next week, okay?"

"Of course, Sarah. And please give my best to Landon. It's a pity he couldn't be here. Malcolm always enjoys his company."

6

"Yes, Landon really wanted to come tonight, but I'm afraid his business trip to Paris is taking longer than expected."
Sarah kisses Estelle on the cheek then crosses the room and says goodbye to Malcolm.

Exercise 1: Definition matching. Ordnen Sie die Definitionen zu!

1. ☐ be better than usual   **a)** keep up appearances

2. ☐ drink just a little bit   **b)** enjoy someone's company

3. ☐ make things seem alright   **c)** outdo oneself

4. ☐ like spending time with someone   **d)** take a sip

Half an hour later, the rest of the guests are gone, too. Estelle is blowing out the last candles when Malcolm comes over and puts an arm around her shoulders. Estelle pushes it away angrily. Malcolm is a little drunk, though, and tries again.
"Estelle, please. Don't be this way. Let's sit together a bit and talk about the party, just like in the old days."
"The old days are over, Malcolm, and you know why. Good night."
Malcolm's brown eyes are a little sad as he watches Estelle turn away, walk up the stairs and go to her room. They have had separate bedrooms for years now, and he knows it's mostly his fault. He also feels partly responsible for his wife's drinking problem. In his mind, he sees her taking out one of the vodka bottles she keeps hidden in her room.

7

She'll be drunk soon, he thinks.

He shrugs and goes over to the bar. It's late – already 1 a.m. – but he decides to have a nightcap anyway. Malcolm wishes now that he had said yes to Lisa's suggestion. She wanted them to meet later after Estelle was in bed.

Just then, the front doorbell rings. Malcolm knows it's foolish, but his first thought is that it could be Lisa. This idea excites him. He almost runs to the front door and doesn't even look to see who's there before he opens it. The person standing outside in the cold November rain is not his sexy assistant, though.

"Hello Malcolm. Happy Birthday," the man says softly. "It's been a long time. You've hardly changed at all."

Exercise 2: Adjectives. Lesen Sie weiter und setzen Sie die fehlenden Adjektive richtig ein!

expensive   black   thick   wet   long   yellow

At first Malcolm just stares at the man. He's tall and wearing a **1.** _____ , dark raincoat. His head is partly covered with a **2.** _____ , waterproof hat, he is wearing **3.** _____ leather gloves and there's a big, **4.** _____ rucksack hanging over his shoulder. He's got some kind of **5.** _____ , wooden cane in his right hand. The left one is holding a bottle of **6.** _____ single-malt whisky.

Then Malcolm focuses on the man's cold, dark-blue eyes. Something about them is familiar, they look like...

Oh my God! It is! It's really him!

"Aren't you going to ask me to come in?" the man asks. "It's bloody cold out here. I'm chilled to the bone."

Malcolm is shocked. He really just wants to close the door, but his political instincts take over. I need to find out why he's here – and what he wants, he thinks.

to shrug	mit den Achseln zucken
nightcap	*hier*: Absacker, Schlummertrunk
foolish	albern, dumm
softly	*hier*: leise
cane	Gehstock
⚡ bloody	verflucht, verdammt
chilled to the bone	*hier*: völlig durchgefroren
to regret	bedauern
inadequate	unzureichend, unangemessen
to drop by	vorbeischauen
for old times' sake	um der alten Zeiten willen

"Yes, certainly, do come inside," Malcolm says. "I'm sorry, but it's just such a surprise to see you again. How have you been?"

Malcolm regrets asking that question the moment the words leave his mouth. They sound so inadequate.

However, the man doesn't seem to think so. He smiles at Malcolm and uses the cane to help him walk slowly through the door and into the townhouse.

"Oh, I'm fine, Malcolm. In fact, I've never been better. And don't worry, I won't stay long. I'm in London on business and thought I'd drop by for old times' sake. I've brought you this. Here."

The man holds out the bottle and Malcolm takes it.

"Oh, well, thank you. Um, why don't I get us a drink? That will help you warm up. You can hang your coat up right there," Malcolm tells him and points to a coat stand.

"Oh, that's kind of you, Malcolm. Very kind."

Malcolm turns to go towards the bar. In that moment, the mysterious man brutally smashes his cane down on Malcolm's head. The MP doesn't even have time to realize what's happening before the cane comes down again. Malcolm falls to the floor, unconscious and bleeding heavily from his head.

The man watches for a moment as the Persian carpet beside Malcolm's head starts to turn red. Then he hits Malcolm again, and again, and again.

Finally, the killer stops. The MP must be dead now, but he checks to be sure. No pulse, no breathing. The killer's heart is racing and he can hear his own ragged breath. He wants to cry out in rage – and triumph. But he hasn't got time to celebrate. There are still too many things to do.

Exercise 3: Unscramble the verbs. **Lesen Sie weiter und bilden Sie sinnvolle Verben aus dem Buchstabensalat!**

First he **1. lkaws** _____ around the room

and **2. lgteh-rihs** _____ some of the

candles. Then he **3. rsutn** _____ off the

electric lights and **4. ekhcsc** _____ that all

the curtains are closed. He **5. enroigs** _____

Malcolm's body – for now – and silently starts to

6. lmcib _____ the stairs to Estelle's

room.

Just as he expected, Estelle is sleeping like a baby on top of the bed. An empty glass is lying next to her. A lamp on the bedside table is still on. Next to it, there's a half-empty bottle of vodka. He watches her for a moment and thinks about killing her, too. But that's not why he's here, so he quietly leaves the room.

to smash	niederschmettern
unconscious	bewusstlos
ragged breath	stoßweißer, unregelmäßiger Atem
blade	Klinge
handle	Griff
gruesome	grausig, grauenhaft
faint	blass, schwach
picture frame	Bilderrahmen
to blink	blinzeln

On his way back down the stairs, the killer reaches into one of the pockets of his coat and takes out an axe blade. It fits perfectly on the end of his 'cane' that really is an axe handle. The murderer touches the blade lightly with one of his gloved fingers and smiles. At the bottom of the stairs, he kisses the axe gently. Then he begins the truly gruesome part of his plan.

When he has finished, he looks carefully at his work.

Yes, he thinks, all the details are perfect.

He takes off his blood-covered clothes and boots and gets clean ones out of his rucksack. After he's changed his clothes, he packs the axe blade, the bottle of whisky and his other things into the rucksack. Finally, he blows out all but one of the candles. Its faint light shines on the empty, heart-shaped picture frame he has placed on the piano.

He looks at the frame, and in his mind he can see the photo that should be inside it. He feels tears start to burn behind his eyes and blinks them away impatiently.

"No!" He says loudly. "I've cried enough. But *they* haven't. Not yet."

11

Exercise 4: True or false? Welche Aussagen sind korrekt? Markieren Sie mit richtig ✔ oder falsch – !

1. Malcolm knows immediately who the man at the door is. ☐
2. The killer tells Malcolm he is not very well. ☐
3. The killer is not surprised that Estelle is asleep. ☐
4. The killer is in a hurry. ☐

Early the next morning, Helen Evans is humming "God Save the Queen" as she walks past Buckingham Palace. Helen is the Ashworth's housekeeper and on her way to the townhouse in nearby Eaton Place. She could take a more direct way, but Helen enjoys going past the palace. She likes to imagine the Queen inside doing something really ordinary – like brushing her teeth or blowing her nose – just like normal people do.

At this hour on a Saturday morning, there isn't much traffic and very few people are out in the nasty weather. When Helen reaches the Ashworth's home, she uses her key to open a small door that leads directly from the street into the ground floor. That's where the kitchen, laundry room and breakfast room are. Normally, Helen has weekends off. She's only at work today because of Mr Ashworth's birthday party last night. She puts her umbrella and coat away and calls out hello. No one answers, but that's not a surprise. Mrs Ashworth often sleeps late, and because of the party, Helen thinks Mr Ashworth is having a lie-in, too.

Helen looks around the kitchen and is glad to see that the catering service has left everything clean and tidy. Since there isn't much work for her to do here, she decides to check the big room upstairs.

For the rest of her life, Helen will never forget what she finds there. The sight that meets her eyes is so horrible and surreal that for a moment, Helen is paralyzed. Something dark red, almost black, is everywhere: on the walls, the curtains, the carpets. But that's not the worst part.

to hum	summen
to imagine	sich vorstellen
ordinary	normal, gewöhnlich
nasty	fies, eklig
laundry room	Waschküche
to have a lie-in	ausschlafen
paralyzed	(wie) gelähmt
pulpy	breiig
mess	Durcheinander, Sauerei
stump	Stumpf, Stummel

Helen sees MP Malcolm Ashworth tied to a chair in front of the piano. His arms – what's left of them – are on the keyboard, which is covered in blood, too. The back of the MP's head is a bloody, pulpy mess. He's not wearing any trousers and the ends of his legs are red stumps. His feet are gone.

Exercise 5: Personal pronouns. Lesen Sie weiter und ergänzen Sie die fehlenden Personalpronomen!

Helen stares at **1.** _____ and presses both hands over **2.** _____ mouth to stop **3.** _____ from screaming. For a moment, **4.** _____ thinks about going upstairs to check on **5.** _____ employer. But what if whoever did this is still here?

13

survival instinct	Selbsterhaltungstrieb
plump	mollig, rundlich
elderly	älter, ältlich
hardly	kaum
to butcher	(ab)schlachten
controversial	umstritten
old-fashioned	altmodisch

Helen's survival instinct takes over. She turns and runs down the stairs as fast as her plump legs will carry her. The only thought racing through her mind now is to get out, get out, get out! Tears are running down her face and as soon as she reaches the street, she finally starts screaming.

Across the street, elderly Lewis Baxter is walking his black Labrador in the rain. When he sees – and hears – Helen, he comes over to her immediately.

"Now, now love, what's wrong? Are you hurt?" he asks.

Helen tries to calm down, but she can hardly speak.

"Police. Need the police. Oh please, sir. Call them now."

"But can you tell me why? What has happened?"

Helen doesn't want to say the words out loud, but she must.

"MP Malcolm Ashworth is... he's dead. Murdered. No, someone has butchered him. And Mrs Ashworth... I, I don't know..."

Lewis Baxter doesn't need to hear anymore. He recognizes the name Malcolm Ashworth. The controversial MP is very well-known. Lewis thinks quickly, then pulls out his old-fashioned mobile phone. He doesn't call 999, the emergency number for New Scotland Yard. Instead, he punches the button

New Scotland Yard ist das Hauptquartier der Polizei im Großraum London. The Metropolitan Police Service wird auch „the Met," „Scotland Yard" oder „The Yard" genannt." Dienstgrade der britischen Polizei sind u.a.:

Detective Sergeant (DS)	Polizeimeister(in)
Detective Inspector (DI)	Kriminalkommissar(in)
Detective Chief Inspector (DCI)	Hauptermittler(in)

14

that will automatically ring his nephew, Detective Chief Inspector Quinn Baxter.

"Well, good morning, Uncle Lewis," Quinn answers sleepily after a few rings.

"No, Quinn, it's not. It's bad, very bad," Lewis tells him.

forensics	Spurensicherung, Kriminaltechnik
ASAP (as soon as possible)	so schnell wie möglich
nightmare	Albtraum
knock-out drops *pl*	K.o.-Tropfen

Then he explains what he's just learnt. "You need to get a team of your best officers and forensics people over here ASAP. And Quinn, from what the housekeeper has told me, you're going to need a profiler, too. A good one."

Exercise 6: Opposite adjectives. Wählen Sie das gegenteilige Adjektiv aus!

1. ☐ plump   a) thin   b) round
2. ☐ old-fashioned   a) traditional   b) modern
3. ☐ elderly   a) young   b) old
4. ☐ well-known   a) unknown   b) famous

Just down the street, the murderer finishes packing his things and looks at his watch again. It's almost time for him to check out of the small but luxurious hotel. He's waiting, though, until the police arrive at the townhouse.

It's a pity about the housekeeper, he thinks. She'll have nightmares for years, poor thing. I wanted Estelle to wake up earlier and find Malcolm – or what's left of him. I guess I put too many knock-out drops in her vodka.

study	Arbeitszimmer
investigator	Ermittler
crime scene	Tatort
mutilated	verstümmelt
coroner	Rechtsmediziner
to chill sb. to the bone	jmd. bis ins Mark erschüttern
disoriented	desorientiert, verwirrt

The murderer looks down at his laptop. The screen shows the live pictures from the four tiny cameras he hid inside the townhouse weeks ago. One of them shows Estelle's room, another is in Malcolm's study and two are placed in the large first floor room. One of those shows a close-up of Malcolm's body. The other one gives a wider view of the entire room.

It's a pity I have to turn them off, he thinks. But first I want to see the investigators so I know who I'll be "working" with. Hmm... I wonder how long it will take them to find the cameras. Finally, he hears sirens. The next part of the show is about to start.

DCI Quinn Baxter has seen a lot of horrible crime scenes in his 30 years with the Metropolitan Police. They are one reason why his thick hair is already completely grey. But the brutality he sees here in the Ashworth home is by far the worst. He looks again at the MP's mutilated body just as the coroner takes another picture of it. The flash from Phillip Tong's camera lights up Malcolm's handless arms on the blood-covered keyboard. The sight chills DCI Baxter to the bone.

But at least Mrs Ashworth will be okay, he tells himself.

An hour ago the first officers on the scene had found her safe but unconscious in her room. It had been hard to wake her, and she was still very disoriented.

A doctor is upstairs with her now. One of the next things on DCI Baxter's long list of things to do is to interview her.

"Quinn?" Inspector Hannah McGowan interrupts his thoughts.

16

Exercise 7: Correct the mistakes. Lesen Sie weiter und korrigieren Sie die sechs Fehler im folgenden Absatz!

"The BIA is finally hear. Do you want to talk too him befour he comes in?"

"Where is it this time?"

Inspector McGowan isn't quiet sure how to give the DCI the bad news. She doesn't have to. Baxter sees the answer on her face.

"Don't tell me. It's that arrogant arse Sheridan, is it?"

1. _____   4. _____

2. _____   5. _____

3. _____   6. _____

"Now, now, Baxter. That really is the pot calling the kettle black," Clay Sheridan smiles as he says this.

He and DCI Quinn Baxter go back a long way.

"Dr Sheridan, I told you to wait downstairs," Inspector McGowan tells him angrily.

"It's all right, Hannah. Clay never listens to anyone else."

BIA (Behavioural Investigative Advisor)	psychologischer Fallanalytiker
the pot calling the kettle black	ein Esel schimpft den anderen Langohr
to go back a long way	sich schon lange kennen

17

to take sth. in	etw. in Augenschein nehmen, erfassen
to stand out	auffallen, hervorstechen
to remind sb. of sth.	jdn. an etw. erinnern
stage	Bühne
victim	Opfer
threat	Drohung
constable	Streifenpolizist
to commit a crime	ein Verbrechen begehen

And DCI Baxter doesn't have time for arguments. Personally, he dislikes Clay Sheridan. But professionally, he knows that Sheridan is one of England's best behavioural investigative advisers.

"Okay, Clay. Where do you want to start?"

But as usual, the profiler isn't listening to him. His eyes are slowly taking in the crime scene one detail at a time. He closes his eyes for a moment to see which image of the crime scene stands out the most. It's a tactic he's used often over the years. This time, what he sees reminds him of a stage in the theatre. Yes, that's it.

"Whoever did this arranged the scene very carefully. They want us to know something – something about the victim and why he was killed in this way. Baxter, I imagine you have already talked to the Home Office. ⓘ Do they have any ideas?"

"Right now, no. Ashworth hadn't received any threats that they know of. But they're still checking..."

"Let me go, I need to see him!"

The sound of Estelle Ashworth's hysterical cries cut off Quinn's words. She's at the top of the stairs trying to get past the doctor and a constable.

Quinn signals the two men to let her come down. He's almost certain that she didn't commit

Das **Home Office** ist das britische Innenministerium, das u.a. zuständig ist für die Innere Sicherheit und die Bekämpfung von Verbrechen und Terrorismus.

18

the crime. In fact, it's hard for him to believe that any woman could have done this, at least not without help. Part of him wants to spare her the gruesome scene.

The other part wants to see her reaction.

The killer is very pleased with the team of investigators inside the townhouse. It's fascinating to watch their responses to his work.

I'm delighted that both Quinn Baxter and Clay Sheridan are involved, he thinks. Those two will be excellent adversaries! Dr Tong is also a very competent coroner. I don't recognize the female inspector, though.

to spare sb. sth.	jmd. etw. ersparen
delighted	entzückt, erfreut
adversary	Gegner
It's worth it.	Es lohnt sich.
temptation	Versuchung
to faint	ohnmächtig werden

I'll have to check her out online tomorrow. Oh I'd love to stay longer, but I need to be gone before the police start questioning the neighbours.

But then he hears Estelle shouting and decides to risk just a few more minutes. It's worth it. He watches with delight as she slowly comes down the stairs.

Normally, Estelle is very careful with her appearance. But now her shoulder-length white hair is a mess and her make-up is smeared. She's having trouble walking, too, and has to hold on to the stairwell.

The temptation to see her face close up is too much for him. He hits the button that controls the zoom on the hidden camera and is just in time to see a look of complete horror come into her grey-blue eyes. Then they fill with tears before she closes them and falls to the floor. She has fainted.

Exercise 8: Translation quiz. Übersetzen Sie und enträtseln Sie das Lösungswort!

1. Mitleid ☐ _ _ _

2. Albtraum _ _ _ _ _ _ _ ☐ _

3. Gerichtsmediziner _ ☐ _ _ _ _ _ _

4. Schuld ☐ _ _ _ _ _

5. Absacker _ ☐ _ _ _ _ _ _

6. Handschuhe _ ☐ _ _ _ _ _

7. Klinge _ _ _ _ _ ☐

8. Gegner _ _ _ _ _ ☐ _ _ _ _

   Lösung: ☐☐☐☐☐☐☐☐

2 KILLER COMMUNICATION

The doctor **rushes** to Estelle and starts checking for her pulse. The investigative and forensic teams stop their activities for a moment. Everyone is staring at Estelle – everyone but Inspector McGowan, that is. Hannah is looking at the ceiling. Then she goes over to DCI Baxter and signals for Clay Sheridan to join them.

"Did you hear it, too?" Hannah whispers to them.

"What?" the two men say **in unison**.

They turn towards each other, both are **frowning**.

"A faint noise coming from up there," Hannah says quietly.

She points quickly at a gold and crystal **chandelier** that is hang-

to rush	eilen, hetzen
in unison	gleichzeitig
to frown	die Stirn runzeln
chandelier	Kronleuchter
⚡ perp (perpetrator)	Täter

ing over the centre of the room. She is still whispering, but she can't keep the excitement out of her voice.

"It sounded like a zoom, definitely some technical noise. We need to search for cameras!"

"But that means the **perp** could be watching us right now!" the profiler whispers back and smiles at Hannah. "That's excellent work, Inspector!"

21

Exercise 9: Verb forms. Lesen Sie weiter und setzen Sie die Verben in der richtigen Form ein!

mean   question   want   try   add   set up

"Yes, Hannah, good job," Quinn **1.** _____ . "It also **2.** _____ the perp may even still be close by. Hannah, have officers **3.** _____ a **road block** at both ends of the street. I **4.** _____ them **5.** _____ every person who **6.** _____ to leave the area. And Jason Foster should begin the **house-to-house enquiries** right now."

Clay Sheridan shakes his head. "Well, you can try it, Baxter. But we don't have any idea who we are looking for. And the murderer carefully planned the whole thing, he or she wouldn't have drawn **undue** attention to themselves."

"That's true, Quinn," Hannah agrees. "And... well, modern cameras can send and receive signals across wide distances. The killer could be just about anywhere."

"I know that! We have to try anyway, Hannah. Besides, a road block will at least keep the reporters away from the scene. They are sure to learn about Ashworth's death soon."

Hannah leaves to follow his orders. Sheridan, though, suddenly has another idea. He walks towards the chandelier and smiles up at it before he speaks.

22

"You're enjoying yourself, aren't you? And you think you are so very clever. But you're not." Clay's voice fills with fake pity. "Poor thing. You've made mistakes – stupid, careless ones. You're a coward, too. You made sure Ashworth was dead before you..."

road block	Straßensperre
house-to-house enquiries *pl*	Anwohner-befragung
undue	*hier*: ungewollt
fake	falsch, unecht
careless	nachlässig, achtlos
coward	Feigling
to grab	packen, greifen

"That's enough, Sheridan!" DCI Baxter shouts angrily as he comes up to Clay and grabs him from behind.

The murderer[i] isn't angry, though. He's laughing.

What a cheap tactic, he thinks. Sheridan wants to make me angry – and keep me watching until the police come. It won't work, though. I'll "talk" to you soon, Sheridan – and that's a promise! He turns off his laptop and packs it away. He's still smiling as he picks up his baggage and goes quickly to the hotel's reception. "Good morning, sir," the receptionist says politely. "Are you ready to check out?"

Achtung, **murder** bedeutet nicht „Mörder", sondern „Mord" oder „ermorden". Die Übersetzung von „Mörder" ist **murderer**, z.B.: *The murderer confessed to the murder of his wife, but still denies murdering her lover.*

"Yes, I am and no, I didn't take anything else from the mini-bar," he tells her before she can ask. "Here's my key card."

He waits while the woman prepares his bill, then he pays it in cash.

"Well, sir, here's your change – and your passport. I hope you enjoyed your stay."

"Yes, everything was lovely, perfect. But I'm afraid I must be on my way now," he adds before she can say anything else.

23

Exercise 10: Police work. Vervollständigen Sie die Sätze mit den passenden Vokabeln für Polizeiarbeit!

1. To check cars and trucks, police set up a r

2. Police use house-to-house e to question...

3. ... people who live near a c s .

4. Police officers must follow their DCI's o .

Three hours later, DCI Baxter is sitting at his desk in New Scotland Yard. He's making notes with one hand and holding a ham and cheese sandwich in the other. Quinn is very thin. His wife, Betty, says he's all skin and bones. She's always telling him to eat more. But right now, the thought of food turns his stomach. He puts the sandwich down just as someone knocks on his door. "Come in," he calls out.

It's Hannah. Her brown eyes look tired.

"Quinn? The Murder Investigation Team[i] is all here now."

"Sheridan, too?"

"Yes, he's arrived. Um, Quinn, can the two of you work together?"

> **Murder Investigation Teams** (MIT) sind spezialisierte Mordkommissionen innerhalb der Londoner Polizei. Jedes der ca. 25 MITs ist für einen bestimmten Stadtbezirk zuständig.

24

Like the rest of the team, Hannah knows about the big argument between Quinn and the profiler at the crime scene. Quinn had even threatened to take Sheridan off the case.

"Yes, I can. He promised not to step out of line again.

They walk in silence down the corridor towards the incident room.

to turn one's stomach	jmd. den Magen umdrehen
case	Fall
to step out of line	aus der Reihe tanzen
incident room	Einsatzzentrale
inappropriate	unangemessen
to brief sb.	jmd. kurz informieren
grisly	grausig, grässlich

Quinn punches in the code that opens the door and holds it open for Hannah to go in first. The other MIT members are already inside talking together quietly. Hannah takes the empty seat next to Clay Sheridan. He smiles at her again and for the first time Hannah notices how attractive he is. She pushes the inappropriate thought out of her mind.

"Thank you all for coming in on a Sunday," DCI Baxter says to open the meeting, "but the Home Office has named this case as the Met's top priority – if needed, with support from M15. To start, I've asked Hannah to brief you about what we know so far. Then our BIA, Dr Clay Sheridan, will give us his first thoughts about the person or people who did this."

Quinn points to the grisly crime scene photos hanging behind him.

Hannah stands up and goes over to the pictures.

"You can see for yourselves what was done to the victim, Member of Parliament from Sheffield Central, Malcolm Ashworth. The coroner will begin the autopsy sometime this afternoon."

Hannah goes back to the table and picks up some papers.

"Here's a summary of what Dr Tong told me at the scene."

Exercise 11: Complete the summary. Lesen Sie weiter und setzen Sie die fehlenden Wörter ein!

perp(s)   weapon   stumps   wounds   mutilated

estimated

1. _____ time of death: between 2:00 and 4:00 a.m.

Cause of death: Severe head 2. _____.

Possible 3. _____: heavy, wooden object.

Other injuries: (post mortem!) 4. _____ arms and legs, only 5. _____ remain, hands and feet not at scene!

6. _____: Most likely strong male, taller than victim.

Everyone has a look at the summary as Hannah continues her report.

"We haven't interviewed the victim's wife yet. Estelle Ashworth is in hospital being treated for shock. Her doctor also believes she either took, or was given, some kind of drug. We're waiting for test results about that – and about these."

Hannah is pointing to another one of the photos. It shows the four tiny cameras police have found hidden in the Ashworth home.

"We are almost certain that the perp placed them there. At this point, we can't say how or when it was done."

26

"Doreen, do you have any new information about the cameras?" Hannah asks the MIT's HOLMES 2 [i] Support Manager.

"No, not really. My assistant is still checking to see if such cameras have been used in other crimes. And related to that, we've also started running the HOLMES cross index for any similar crimes involving axes and, um, missing hands and feet."

"Excuse me," Clay interrupts. "Doreen, make sure to also check for missing fingers and/or toes. The perp may have started less radically."

HOLMES 2 (Home Office Large Major Enquiry System) ist die 2. Version einer Datenbank, die die britische Polizei für Ermittlungen und zum Katastrophenmanagement benutzt. Der Name ist eine Anspielung auf Sherlock Holmes, den berühmten britischen Privatdetektiv.

It's a good point, but before Hannah can thank him, her mobile phone rings. She looks at the display and takes the call. It's Jason Foster, the team's House-to-House Coordinator. She listens for a moment, then suddenly the tiredness disappears from her eyes. "And has the room been cleaned, yet?" Hannah asks. "No? Then make sure no one goes inside it before forensics gets there."

She listens while Officer Foster gives her more details. "What! That's unbelievable. We're on our way."

Hannah ends the call and turns to the team. "We've got a hot lead on the killer! Jason is at a hotel on Eaton Street. The receptionist there says a tall guest from the United States named David Smith checked out quickly this morning. And Clay, I mean Dr Sheridan..."

male	hier: Mann
cross index	Querverweis
hot lead	heiße Spur

"You can call me Clay, Hannah," the profiler tells her.

27

For some reason, Hannah feels her face turning pink at his words. But there's no time for her to think about why.

"Clay, the man left an envelope with the receptionist. It has your name on it!"

The killer looks at his watch and sighs in relief. The drive north along the motorway M1 has taken just over three hours. But he's on schedule.

Exercise 12: American to British. Lesen Sie weiter und ersetzen Sie die amerikanischen Wörter mit ihren britischen Entsprechungen!

He turns off the 1. highway _____ and soon sees the golf 2. center _____ in Rother Valley, just outside Sheffield. Compared to rainy London, it's a fine, 3. fall _____ day here in South Yorkshire. That means the golf course 4. parking lot _____ is quite full. But he finds a spot for the silver rental car, parks and turns off the 5. engine _____. He checks again that the items in his 6. pants' _____ pockets are ready. Then he gets out of the car and opens its 7. trunk _____.

He would like to see how Malcolm's hands and feet are doing. That's too risky here, though. So he just makes sure the cool box holding them is still closed properly. He smiles when he thinks about what he will soon be adding to the box. Then he takes out a golf bag and puts it over his shoulder. It's heavy, but he hardly notices. He begins humming his favourite song as he starts walking.

In nearby Norwood, 68-year old Neal Walsh is busy making shelves for the workshop in the garage of his weekend cottage. It's so wonderful to be retired and have time for such projects, he thinks. He pushes another piece of wood through a table saw and inhales deeply. Oh, how I love the scent of freshly cut wood. But wait, I can smell something else, something strange and sweet...

to sigh in relief	erleichtert seufzen
item	Gegenstand
cottage	kleines Landhaus
retired	pensioniert
scent	Duft, Geruch
to struggle	kämpfen
former	ehemalig
Lord Mayor	Oberbürgermeister
to drag	ziehen, schleppen

Before Neal has time to identify the smell, he feels hands grabbing him from behind and someone is pressing a handkerchief over his mouth and nose.

Don't breathe! Neal tells himself as he starts struggling. Maybe I can force the attacker's arm into the saw.

But Neal isn't strong enough. The attacker pulls him away from the saw and holds on tightly until Neal finally has to take a breath. Seconds later, Sheffield's former Lord Mayor is unconscious.

Chloroform wears off quickly. So, the murderer is careful to keep the handkerchief over Neal's mouth while he drags him to an armless, wooden chair in the other corner of the garage. Then he binds the older man's hands and feet to the chair with plastic

29

cable ties and replaces the handkerchief with a gag. The killer sees Neal start to open his eyes. He backs away and turns off the saw. The killer enjoys the complete silence for a moment. Then Neal starts moaning from behind the gag.

Exercise 13: Fill in the blanks. Lesen Sie weiter und setzen Sie die Begriffe richtig ein!

wearing   widen   sick   disoriented   happening

Neal feels 1. _____ and 2. _____.

Why can't I move? What's 3. _____? Why...

Then he sees the tall man 4. _____ a black ski mask. Neal's eyes 5. _____ with fear.

"If you promise not to scream, I will remove the gag. Later." Neal shakes his head and tries to say the word yes. His thoughts are racing and he is trying not to panic completely. Who is this man? What does he want with me? What is he going to do to me? The killer goes over to his golf bag and removes a video camera. After he sets it up on a tripod, he looks through the lens. Yes,

cable ties *pl*	Kabelbinder
gag	Knebel
to moan	stöhnen
tripod	Stativ
to suffer	leiden
tatty	abgegriffen, zerfleddert

Neal Walsh seems to be suffering. Then he takes a small book out of the bag. The brown paper cover is old and tatty. He holds up the book so that Neal can see it.

"Do you know what this is? Have you ever seen it before?"

Neal shakes his head again, this

30

time meaning no, and manages to choke out something that almost sounds like "please, please."

The stranger opens the book. "It's funny that you don't recognize it. Part of it is about you – and what you did. With Malcolm Ashworth and..."

He stops speaking. Neal has started to rock the chair back and forth, which makes the killer laugh. Neal thought he couldn't be more terrified. But those words – and the man's crazy laugh – cut him to the bone. He's starting to understand.

to choke out	erstickt sagen
to rock	schaukeln
back and forth	vor und zurück
to cut sb. to the bone	jmd. tief treffen
spirit	*hier*: Mut, Kampfgeist
to right sth.	etw. aufrichten
to strangle	erwürgen
This is it.	Das war's dann.

Suddenly, the chair crashes to the floor. It doesn't break, but Neal's spirit does.

"I'll help you up, Lord Mayor," the man says almost gently as he rights the chair. "Oh, your head's bleeding. Here, let me help."

He slowly takes off his mask and lets Neal look into his eyes. The two men stare at each other until the killer places the mask over Neal's head – backwards. Now Neal can't see anything, but he can feel the man's hands reaching under the mask.

He's going to strangle me, Neal thinks. This is it. I'll never see Julie or our girls again, or get to hold my first grandchild. Neal feels as if his heart is about to explode. There are tears in his eyes now, which are falling on the killer's hands.

"Lord Mayor? Why are you crying? I only want to do this."

In that moment, the killer suddenly removes the gag. The shock of it makes Neal scream, and the killer hits him in the stomach.

"You promised not to scream. Now follow the rules. My rules."

"Who are you?" Neal whispers. "And what do want of me?"
"I want you to tell me the truth about that night. All of it."

Exercise 14: Questions about the text. Beantworten Sie die Fragen zum Text!

1. Is Neal Walsh the Lord Mayor of Sheffield?

   _____

2. Does Neal know Malcolm Ashworth?

   _____

3. Is Neal a grandfather?

   _____

4. Does the killer want to kill Neal now?

   _____

"Wait. Stop it for a moment, please," Hannah asks Clay and Quinn. The three of them are back in the incident room, staring in horror at what David Smith had left for Clay at the hotel. It's a video saved on a flash drive[i] and it shows every detail of Malcolm Ashworth's murder – and what the killer did to him afterwards.

"Look, right there," Hannah continues. "Right after he puts the frame on the piano, his shoulders start shaking. Is he crying?"

Vorsicht mit englischen Wörtern in der deutschen Sprache! Auf Englisch sagt man nicht „USB Stick" sondern **flash drive.** Ein anderes Beispiel ist „Handy", was nur auf Deutsch „Mobiltelefon" bedeutet. Auf Englisch bedeutet **handy** einfach „handlich" oder „praktisch".

"Could be," Clay tells her. "It's hard to say, though. He's been very careful to keep his face away from the cameras. That shows he has a certain degree of self control."

He sees how upset Hannah

certain degree	gewisser Grad, gewisses Maß
pointedly	*hier*: demonstrativ
surveillance	Überwachung
angle	*hier*: Ermittlungs-ansatz, Blick-winkel

is and puts a hand on her shoulder. "Hannah, are you okay?"
"Yeah, I'm fine. It's just, this bloody psychopath is playing with us!"
"You're right, Hannah," Quinn speaks up.
He looks pointedly at the profiler's hand on her shoulder and Hannah stands up suddenly.

Exercise 15: Present Simple or Present Progressive?
Lesen Sie weiter und unterstreichen Sie die richtige Variante!

"Um, Quinn, can you tell us what the rest of the team members **1.** do / are doing ?" she asks quickly.

"Some **2.** look / are looking through the hotel surveillance camera recordings for photos of David Smith. Others **3.** are checking / check out the passport angle. That **4.** needs / is needing time, though. Doreen **5.** is preparing / prepares a background report on Ashworth. Let's hope it **6.** is helping / helps ."

⚡ pissed off	stinksauer, angepisst
revenge	Rache
remote control	Fernbedienung
eerie	unheimlich
clue	Hinweis, Indiz
to exclaim	(überrascht) ausrufen

"Among other things, we have to find out details about his political positions," Quinn continues. "Maybe that's what got him killed."

"Oh come on, Baxter. Does it seem as if the killer is pissed off about politics? To me, this crime screams of something else: hate – and revenge."

"Well, Sheridan, as you said this morning, we have to check it out," Quinn says, referring to their argument. "But Doreen is also investigating Ashworth's financial records and private life. And I have other team members out interviewing the party guests as well."

"Okay, Baxter. I'm sorry, I know you are just doing your job. Let's see the rest now. Maybe the killer left a message for us at the end."

Quinn hits the play button on the remote control and they watch the rest of the video in silence. It's eerie for them to see themselves appear on the screen. When they reach the part where the camera starts to zoom in on Estelle, Clay cries out.

"Look at her eyes! It's just like I told him. The killer made a mistake – and he's given us a clue."

"What?" Hannah exclaims.

"See?" Clay exclaims and puts the video in slow motion. "First her eyes focus on her husband in front of the piano, but then they turn a little. She's looking at something else just before she faints."

"But what?" Hannah asks as the camera zooms out again.

"That," Quinn says and points to the heart-shaped frame.

34

Exercise 16: Crossword puzzle. Lösen Sie das Kreuzworträtsel!

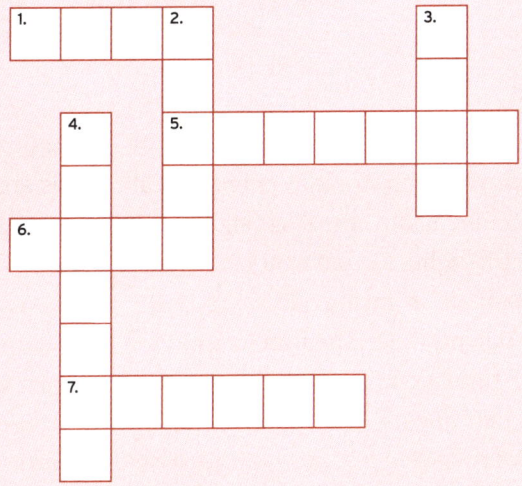

Across

1. If you follow orders, you don't step out of …
5. Clay thinks this could be the perp's motive.
6. Angry words can cut someone to the …
7. You don't "do" a crime, you … one.

Down

2. Something strange and unnatural is …
3. A sound that can signal relief or tiredness
4. Gruesome things can turn your …

3 BARE BONES

"I don't know what you mean…"

Another punch to his stomach cuts off Neal's words abruptly.

"Don't lie to me again!" the killer shouts.

"All right, all right. I'll tell you, but…," Neal is thinking desperately, "but my wife, she'll be home any time now and… and she's bringing guests, too. Lots of them. We're having a…"

punch	Schlag
fist	Faust
madman	Irrer, Verrückter
evilly	böse
to hiss	zischen

The killer smashes his fist directly into Neal's mouth. The pain is so bad Neal is almost sick. But the man's next words hurt much more.

"Your wife Julie is in Bristol. She's visiting one of your daughters until tomorrow. Her name's Margery, isn't it? She's the one who's expecting a baby at the end of next month. The women haven't told you yet, but it's going to be a boy."

Neal is shocked. How can this madman know all these private details about my family? Even things I don't know myself.

"How did you find out all of this?" he asks in a shaky voice.

"Modern technology is a wonderful thing, Lord Mayor. But you – and your lovely wife – don't use it safely. I discovered your passwords easily and have been reading your emails for months now. And I've been watching you, too. All of you," he adds evilly.

Neal's entire body starts shaking now with fear – and rage.

36

"You leave my family alone, you monster!" he hisses.

"Oh, I will, Lord Mayor, I promise. But only if you tell me what I came to find out. If you don't cooperate, perhaps I'll just wait until Julie comes home."

Neal knows he's beaten now. He doesn't trust the man to keep his word, but it's the only chance he has to try and keep his family safe.

Exercise 17: Plurals. Bilden Sie die richtige Pluralform!

1. wife _____

2. technology _____

3. fist _____

4. man _____

In a low voice, he begins talking. When he's finished, Neal is crying again. This time with regret.

"I'm sorry, I'm terribly sorry. Please, let me go now. It was really Malcolm's fault and I never wanted..."

The killer has heard enough.

"Thank you, Lord Mayor, for finally speaking the truth – or at

in a low voice	mit leiser Stimme
regret	Bedauern
to reward sb.	jmd. belohnen
honesty	Ehrlichkeit
merciful	gnädig

least part of it. You must be rewarded for your honesty," he says calmly while he pulls Neal's head up and removes the mask.

For a moment, Neal begins to hope that the man will be merciful. But no, the killer puts the gag back inside his mouth and then pushes Neal's head forwards. That's when he sees the axe and a chopping block next to the golf bag. He begins to whimper.

"By the way, you asked who I am," the killer says as he walks to the centre of the room.

He turns the saw back on and then goes and picks up his axe.

chopping block	Hackklotz
to whimper	wimmern
to twist away	sich wegdrehen
wrist	Handgelenk
to suspect	vermuten
blurry	unscharf, verschwommen

He's shaking with excitement. This time, Sheridan won't be able to call me a coward, he thinks.

He pushes the chair and Neal feels himself falling backwards. He lands hard on his back. In horror, Neal tries to twist away from the chopping block the man is putting under his right hand. But he can't. The man is standing on Neal's right wrist. He knows no one can hear him, but Neal tries to scream for help as the killer slowly raises his axe.

"My name is Vidar," he shouts. Then with all his strength, he swings the axe down.

Estelle Ashworth's hands are shaking. It's late Sunday afternoon and she's lying in bed at the Chelsea and Westminster hospital in London.

"I'm sorry, Mrs Ashworth. I know how horrible this is for you. We're almost finished," Hannah says gently.

The police have been interviewing her for half an hour now. Inspector Hannah McGowan seems nice, but Estelle doesn't want to talk to her anymore. The two men with her are also making Estelle nervous. DCI Baxter and Dr Sheridan haven't said much.

Estelle suspects they think she will talk more openly to a woman. They are wrong.

"So, the name David Smith doesn't mean anything to you?"

"No, I already said that, didn't I?"

"And have you ever seen this man?" Hannah holds up a photo from the hotel surveillance camera.

Exercise 18: Question tags. Lesen Sie weiter und ergänzen Sie die Frageanhängsel!

"I'm sorry, Inspector, but the photo is very blurry, 1. _____ ? So to be honest, I can't be sure, 2. _____ ?"

"No, that's true," said Hannah. "Try this one. It shows him from behind."

"And you think this man killed my husband, 3. _____ ?" Estelle says quietly. "So you should be looking for him, 4. _____ ?"

"We are, Mrs Ashworth. And you will help us, 5. _____ ?"

"Of course. But I don't recognize him. I'm sorry." Estelle replies.

"Okay. But what about this?" Hannah asks and shows Estelle a photo of the heart-shaped picture frame.

Estelle takes it and looks at it carefully. Her hands start to shake a little bit more. "No, I've never seen it before."

encouraging	ermutigend, aufmunternd
faithful	treu
gossip	*hier*: Klatschtante
to imply	andeuten
occasionally	gelegentlich
⚡ fling	Techtelmechtel, kurze Affäre
condolences *pl*	Beileid
to drug sb.	jmd. betäuben, jmd. narkotisieren
to shiver	zittern, schlottern

"Are you certain? It's very important. The killer brought it to your home – and left it there. So it must mean something."

"Well it doesn't! Not to me!" Estelle's voice is getting louder.

Hannah looks over at Clay and he gives her an encouraging look.

"Mrs Ashworth, one of your party guests told us that your husband wasn't always faithful. Is that true?"

"Who said that? Was it that gossip, Sarah Mead?"

"Well, yes, it was. Mrs Mead implied that your husband was having an affair with his assistant, Lisa Giles. How did you feel about that?"

Estelle takes a deep breath to try and calm her nerves. She doesn't want to lose control in front of the police.

"Inspector, Malcolm and I have been – I mean were married for 39 years. If he occasionally looked at – or even had a fling with another woman, I ignored it. If you want to know anything about Malcolm and Ms Giles, ask her, not me. And tell Sarah she should keep an eye on her own husband, not..."

Estelle's voice breaks and her eyes fill with tears. She's remembered that she will never again have to 'keep an eye on' Malcolm.

She brushes the tears away. "Now please, Inspector, if you have more questions, can you come another time? I want to be alone now."

Estelle closes her eyes to signal that the interview is over.

40

"Very well, Mrs Ashworth," Hannah tells her. "We'll see each other tomorrow. I'll leave my card in case you think of anything else we should know before then."

Hannah stands up and so do Clay and Quinn. But before they leave, Quinn goes over to the bed and takes Estelle's hand.

"Mrs Ashworth, once again let me say how very sorry I am for you loss. Please accept my condolences – and my promise. We will find the man who butchered your husband – and drugged you. We will also find out why."

Exercise 19: Opposites match-up. Ordnen Sie die Vokabeln ihrem Gegenteil zu!

1. ☐ fling   **a)** often
2. ☐ blurry   **b)** congratulations
3. ☐ occasionally   **c)** marriage
4. ☐ condolences   **d)** clear

Outside the hospital it is already dark and it's raining again. Hannah shivers a little as she listens to Quinn and Clay talk about the interview with Estelle Ashworth.

"So do you think she's telling us the truth, Sheridan?"

"Partly. I don't think she recognized the photos of David Smith – or whatever his name is. But..."

"She knows something about that picture frame," Quinn interrupts him. "I'm sure of it!"

"Yes, me too," Clay adds. "And I don't think she just ignored his 'occasional flings', as she put it. She doesn't seem the type."

"But do you think she had anything to do with his murder?"

41

"You mean something like hiring a hit man? It's a long shot, but it's possible."

"I'll have Doreen do a background check on Mrs Ashworth, too."

"Good idea, Baxter."

Hannah can hardly believe that her boss and the profiler are speaking to each other so politely. She hopes it means that the relationship between the two men is improving. But this is the wrong time and place to work on relationship-building – Hannah is cold, tired and hungry.

"So, you two, do we have to discuss this here? The Sporting Page is close by. It's quite a nice pub and not too expensive. Why don't we go there for a drink and a bite to eat? While we're there, we can plan our next steps."

"That's an excellent suggestion, Hannah," Quinn tells her.

Exercise 20: Prepositions. Lesen Sie weiter und vervollständigen Sie den Text mit den richtigen Präpositionen!

after   at   for   without   back   on   for

"But I have to drive 1. _____ to the Yard and check 2. _____ the others. And I want to eat 3. _____ home with Betty. I don't think I'll have much time 4. _____ her until 5. _____ this case is solved. But you and Clay go 6. _____ me. We'll see each other 7. _____ a team meeting at 8:00 tomorrow morning."

42

Hannah and Clay wave good-bye to Quinn as he leaves them and walks towards his car. For a moment, Clay is tempted to go with Hannah. It would be nice to have dinner with a very pretty and intelligent woman – and Hannah is certainly that.

hit man	Auftragskiller
long shot	weithergeholte Vermutung
to improve	(sich) verbessern
to be tempted to do sth.	versucht sein, etw. zu tun
starving	am Verhungern
to wonder	*hier*: sich fragen

Funny, I never noticed it before today, he thinks.

"I'm sorry, too, Hannah. But I also need to work tonight."

He sees a strange look on her face. Is it disappointment?

"But can we do it another time? I'd really like that," he adds.

"Sure, Clay, some other time then. But I'm starving now, so I guess I'll go the pub alone. I'll see you tomorrow."

I should just follow her and try and forget about everything for a couple of hours. It would be good for me – but not for her, Clay thinks. And anyway, we would just talk about the case, about the horrible things we've seen today. I wonder where the murderer is now – and what he's doing."

Exercise 21: Implied relationships. Welche Aussagen sind im Text angedeutet? Kreuzen Sie an!

1. Estelle Ashworth is being totally honest with the police. ❐

2. Clay and Hannah are attracted to each other. ❐

3. Sarah Mead's husband might not always be faithful. ❐

4. Quinn and his wife have a good relationship. ❐

Just before 6 a.m. the next morning, Janine Morrison is almost finished with her night shift at the police contact management centre in Sheffield. She is looking forward to going home soon when another call comes through on the 999 emergency number.

"Good morning, South Yorkshire Police. How may I help you?"

"Send someone to Neal Walsh's weekend home ASAP. I think the former Lord Mayor needs help," a male voice says.

The caller hangs up before Janine can ask him for details. She wonders for a moment how to handle the situation. Then she decides to inform her supervisor, Alice Hall, about it.

"It's most likely a crank call, Janine. But it's better to be safe than sorry. Send a patrol car to have a look."

Monday mornings are always hectic at the Tidwell home in the village of Killamarsh. Sylvia Tidwell hurries to make breakfast for her family. It's already half past six. Her husband and grown-up son, who still lives with them, have to leave for work soon.

Exercise 22: Adverb or adjective? Lesen Sie weiter und unterstreichen Sie die richtige Variante!

"Good morning, Mum," 31-year-old Kevin says 1. sleepy / sleepily as he comes into the kitchen and gives her a 2. quick / quickly kiss on the cheek. "Did you sleep 3. good / well ?"

"Yes love, I did. And you? You look 4. tired / tiredly ."

"Yeah, I slept okay. Just stayed up too 5. late / lately . Where's Dad?"

"He's out walking *your* dog."

Just then the two of them hear barking outside. Sylvia opens the door and Kevin's Dachshund runs in and jumps up on his knees.

"Get down, Silky, old girl. Your paws are dirty."

Then Kevin turns to his father. "Thanks for walking Silky, Dad."

The family sits down and Sylvia pours them all some tea. Her

police contact management centre	Telefonbereitschaft der Polizei
supervisor	Vorgesetzte
crank call	Juxanruf
barking	Bellen
Dachshund	Dackel
paw	Pfote
⚡ to do sb. in	jmd. abmurksen
courier	Kurier
special delivery	Eilzustellung, Sonderlieferung
to rattle	rasseln

husband Carl adds sugar to his and opens the morning paper.

"Is there any news about MP Ashworth's murder?" Kevin asks while he butters a slice of toast.

"No, son. The police are holding a news conference later this morning. What a horrible crime, though. Poor man."

"Poor?" Sylvia says sarcastically. "Malcolm Ashworth? I'm just surprised someone didn't do him in years ago."

"Sylvia! You shouldn't say things like that!"

Before Sylvia can respond, the front door bell rings.

"I'll get it," Kevin says and is glad for the interruption.

Kevin looks out the window before he opens the door. There's a tall man wearing a courier's uniform standing outside.

"Morning, sir," he says when Kevin opens the door. "I've got a special delivery for Mr Kevin Tidwell."

"Oh, that's me. Should I sign for it?"

"Yes, right here. Thank you. And have a nice day."

Kevin comes back to the table holding a small packet. He shakes it and smiles when it rattles.

"Look Mum, Dad, it's from grandma."

Silky starts growling while Kevin is opening the packet. And when he looks inside, he gasps in shock. Silky suddenly jumps up and starts trying to bite the small box.

to growl	knurren
to gasp	nach Luft schnappen
freckled	sommersprossig
pale	blass

"What is it, Kevin?" his dad asks.

Kevin's freckled face is pale now. He silently turns the box around so his parents can see the contents. Inside the box there's a gold wedding ring, an envelope and nine small bones.

"Bloody hell," Carl exclaims. "Those look like..."

"Finger bones," Kevin says softly.

Silky begins barking madly as all three of the Tidwell's look at Kevin's left hand. The one that is missing three fingers.

Exercise 23: Hidden words. Finden Sie 10 Geräusche!

G	R	O	W	L	E	O	F	I
H	A	W	H	I	S	P	E	R
L	T	T	I	S	H	B	K	S
O	T	I	M	M	O	A	N	C
X	L	Z	P	R	U	Q	J	R
D	E	T	E	O	T	U	L	E
A	Y	A	R	B	A	R	K	A
G	A	S	P	U	N	T	E	M
E	M	P	W	S	I	G	H	N

46

Clay walks past Big Ben just as the famous bell in the Elizabeth Tower[1] chimes 7 a.m. He looks up at the Palace of Westminster. Normally, he enjoys seeing the impressive building where the House of Commons and House of Lords both meet. But today it troubles him to think that one MP won't be there when this morning's session of Parliament begins. He continues his

to chime	schlagen, läuten
impressive	imposant, beeindruckend
to trouble sb.	jmd. beunruhigen, jmd. Sorgen machen
mood	Laune, Stimmung
revolving	sich drehend
shapely	wohlgeformt
to catch up with sb.	jmd. einholen
to bother sb.	jmd. Sorgen bereiten, jmd. plagen
sharply	spitz, scharf

walk, and eight minutes later he reaches New Scotland Yard. His mood lightens when he sees Hannah just going past the building's famous revolving sign. Today she's wearing a black skirt that ends just above her knees. It shows off her shapely legs. Clay walks faster so he can catch up with her.

"Good morning, Hannah. You're early, too."

"Yes, well, I had too much on my mind and didn't sleep well."

"It was the same with me. This case is really bothering me."

"And did you finish all your work last night?" Hannah asks a little sharply.

Seit 2012 heißt der Turm am Palace of Westminster, in dem die Glocke Big Ben zu Hause ist, „the Elizabeth Tower". Er wurde umbenannt zu Ehren des 60. Thronjubiläums von Queen Elizabeth II. - dem „Diamond Jubilee".

"It took me a long time, but yes. And you? Did you enjoy yourself at the pub?"

"It was very nice, thank you. There was a football match on the TV – and I met a couple of nice people."

Clay wants to ask her more – like if the "nice people" were male

47

security procedures *pl*	Sicherheitsschranken

or female. He decides not to, though.

Then the two of them go through the complicated security procedures to enter the building. When they are done, they both start talking at the same time.

"Clay, I..."

"Hannah, would you..."

They laugh a little nervously and Clay motions for Hannah to go first. But just then her mobile beeps to signal she has received a text message. It's from Quinn. When Hannah reads it, she suddenly goes pale. Silently, she gives her phone to Clay so he can see it too.

Exercise 24: Missing words. Lesen Sie weiter und setzen Sie die fehlenden Wörter in Quinns SMS richtig ein!

ASAP   butchered   message   politician

MIT   victim   incident

To all 1. _____ members. Need you here in 2. _____ room 3. _____ . There has been another murder in Sheffield. 4. _____ also a 5. _____ , Sheffield's former Lord Mayor. Has also been 6. _____ . AND: there's another 7. _____ for Dr Sheridan.

48

4 BONES TO PICK

When Clay and Hannah reach the incident room, Quinn is speaking with Yolanda Tailor, the MIT Office Manager and Zane Jarwar, another of the team's administrators.

"Yolanda, make sure everything is ready for the live conference with the police in South Yorkshire. And Zane, I need your summary of all the information we've received so far."

"When do you need it?" Zane asks.

He looks exhausted.

"Ten minutes ago," Quinn barks.

"I know it's a lot," he adds when he sees Zane's face. "Yolanda, get someone to help Zane."

The two administrators leave the room to follow Quinn's instructions just as the other team members start arriving.

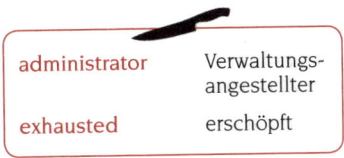

administrator	Verwaltungsangestellter
exhausted	erschöpft

While they are getting seated, Clay goes up to Quinn.

"What was the message, Quinn? Is it another flash drive?"

"No, nothing high-tech this time. He left you a simple note. It was taped to the body – on the victim's right arm. All it says is, 'Tell Dr Clay Sheridan I'll speak with him again soon.'"

The other team members hear Quinn's words and look worried, especially Hannah.

"Quinn, it bothers me that the killer is communicating with Clay."

"Me, too, Hannah. But we'll discuss it during the meeting."

Quinn greets the team. He quickly tells them the second victim's name, how the body was discovered and the few other details he knows about Neal Walsh's murder.

"Right now it looks like we are dealing with the same perp," Quinn concludes. "And because both victims were politicians from Sheffield, I think that's where we have to focus our investigation."

"I need to see the crime scene as quickly as possible," Clay adds.

"*All* of us are going to see it in just a few minutes," Quinn explains.

Exercise 25: Present Perfect clues. Lesen Sie weiter und setzen Sie die Hinweiswörter für das Present Perfect richtig ein!

yet   already   for   just   never

"Yolanda and I have 1. _____ arranged for a video conference. Sheffield's Chief of Police has 2. _____ done a VC from a crime scene before. But Stuart Wells has 3. _____ agreed to let us 'visit' the scene virtually. He hasn't arrived there 4. _____ , but their forensics team has been working 5. _____ about an hour."

"Do they know to look for hidden cameras?" Hannah asks.

"Chief Wells is informed. But I told him *not* to have his team search for cameras. Instead, he's called in a surveillance

50

truck. If the killer is watching again, maybe they can trace the signal."

"That's an excellent plan, Quinn," Clay says approvingly. "And have the Sheffield police got a lead on the person who made the anonymous phone call?"

"No, Clay, but they are assuming it came from the killer himself."

"But why would the killer do that?" Hannah wonders. "It doesn't really make sense."

"It makes sense to him," Clay says. "Just like everything else he's doing – and is going to do."

"What do you mean?" Hannah interrupts. "Do you think...?"

"No, I don't think – I know. His note said he'll talk to me again soon. That means he's not finished. I'm sure he's only just begun."

to greet	begrüßen
Chief of Police	Polizeichef
to trace sth.	etw. (zurück)verfolgen
approvingly	anerkennend
to assume	ausgehen von
chilling	erschreckend, ernüchternd
briefcase	Aktentasche

"Are you saying you believe we're dealing with a serial killer?" Quinn asks sharply.

It's a chilling thought.

"Not in the traditional sense, no. But if you like, I can tell you more about my theory while we're waiting for Chief Wells."

"All right, Clay. It's a good moment to hear your ideas."

Clay nods and takes out some papers from his briefcase.

"Here's a copy of the killer profile I prepared last night. Of course it doesn't include anything about the second murder. But it contains points and questions that I think could help us identify, understand and catch him."

51

Exercise 26: Linking words. Lesen Sie weiter, unter-streichen Sie die Verbindungswörter und bringen Sie Clays Sätze in die richtige Reihenfolge!

a) On the one hand, that says he wants us to *know* him – and maybe stop him.

b) Now let's move on to my list of open questions...

c) Furthermore, he's arrogant and gets a kick out of playing with us – especially me.

d) To start with, it's very unusual that the killer is sharing so much information with us.

e) For example, he's let us *see* his general appearance – and, well, how he does his 'work'.

f) But on the other hand, he has an agenda – a mission that is all about revenge.

1	2	3	4	5	6

Just then, Yolanda comes back inside and tells Quinn that Chief Wells is at the scene and available now. She switches on the large flat screen monitor on the wall that's attached to the VC device and makes sure the recorder is also on.
A short, plump man appears on the screen. He's standing in Neal Walsh's hobby workshop and holding a tablet.

52

"Good morning, Chief Wells," Quinn tells him. "Thank you for contacting us so quickly and agreeing to collaborate with us."

"You're welcome. So can you see me... and the crime scene?" He turns the tablet slowly to the left and the MIT members get

agenda	*hier*: Plan
available	verfügbar
device	Gerät
to collaborate	zusammen-arbeiten
blood stain	Blutfleck
pattern	Muster
evidence	Beweise

their first look at Neal Walsh's body. It is a horrible sight. Quinn waits for a moment to let everyone take it in.

"Can you bring the tablet closer to the body?"

Chief Wells takes a deep breath before he walks over to where the coroner is examining the victim. The tablet starts shaking.

"Sorry, Chief Inspector. It's just that, I know – knew – him well."

"I'm sorry, too, Chief. I'm certain that it's not easy for any of you."

"Yes, well, the coroner just gave me some information based on the blood stain patterns. Neal was most likely already dead before the murderer cut off the feet. But he... he was definitely still alive when the hands were chopped off."

Now the team can see the message taped to Neal's right arm. It's on thick, cream-coloured paper. The letters in the message look as if they have been cut out of a newspaper.

"Chief Wells? This is Clay Sheridan. Can you turn the note over?"

"Sure. Just wait a second while I get the photographer to take another few pictures of this piece of evidence [i] the way it is."

Die sogenannten „unzählbaren Nomen" wie **evidence** haben keine Pluralform und stehen nie mit einem unbestimmten Artikel. Um eine genaue Menge anzugeben, verwendet man Ausdrücke wie **a piece/pieces of** oder **some**. Weitere unzählbare Nomen sind z.B. *information, furniture, advice* oder *traffic*.

53

Exercise 27: New words. Unterstreichen Sie die Wörter, die nicht zu den neuen Vokabeln passen!

1. collaborate	cooperate	appear	teamwork
2. stain	dirt	blood	hobby
3. device	victim	flash-drive	smartphone
4. evidence	fingerprints	crime scene	recorder

When the Chief turns the note over a few moments later, everyone gasps in surprise. A name is on it – written in blood.

"Vidar!" Chief Wells reads the name out loud. "What the devil does that mean?"

Clay's eyes are glowing with excitement.

"It means that I was right about his motive. In Norse mythology, Vidar is the god of silence – and revenge."

"But revenge for what?" Chief Wells asks angrily. "Neal Walsh was a wonderful man – and a very good Lord Mayor."

⚡ What the devil!	Was zum Teufel!
Norse	altnordisch
to have a bone to pick with sb.	mit jmd. ein Hühnchen zu rupfen haben
to curse	*hier*: fluchen
muffled	gedämpft
to scribble	kritzeln
to clench (one's fist)	(die Faust) ballen

"Well, Chief," Quinn says slowly, "the killer clearly had a bone to pick with Neal Walsh, and with Malcolm Ashworth, too – if you'll excuse the expression. We have to find out what it was."

"And who else was involved," Clay reminds them.

The flat-screen monitor in the incident room suddenly goes black. Yolanda curses and gets

54

up to check the cables. Before she reaches them, though, the audio and video return. But it's a different scene. The investigators are now seeing a close-up shot of a pair of light-grey eyes. They are filled with tears – and terror. Slowly, the picture zooms out and the MIT team is now seeing a very elderly man. He's tied to a large leather chair in front of an antique desk. The dark red curtains behind him are closed. The man is gagged and everyone shivers at the sound of his muffled cries.

Only Quinn remains calm enough to act. He quickly scribbles a note to Yolanda. "Get IT security to start tracing the hacker." Yolanda nods and silently leaves the room. She's secretly glad she won't have to see what she is sure is coming next.

Exercise 28: Fill in the blanks. Lesen Sie weiter und unterstreichen Sie die richtige Variante!

But the others are not so 1. lucky / happy . As they look helplessly 2. on / at the screen, the camera zooms in again. 3. It gives / There is a close-up of the 4. man's / men's hand. He 5. is trying / tries to clench it, but he can't – he is 6. to / too weak.

They hear the sound of footsteps on a wooden floor. Then they stop. The man is whimpering louder now and the team can also hear him breathing heavily through his nose. Suddenly, there is another sound. A bell is ringing faintly in the background.

One... two... three... Hannah holds her breath and realizes she is counting the rings. When she gets to eight, the axe falls and blood spurts out of the man's wrist. But it wasn't a clean cut. The man's hand is still half attached to his arm and his fingers are twitching. Then the axe blade falls again and the team hears the killer's mad laughter – and the victim's muffled screams of agony as his hand falls to the floor.

"No!" Hannah can't stop herself from crying out.

Clay is sitting next to her. Without thinking, he takes her hand and holds it gently under the table. Quinn, though, looks at her sharply. The killer has stopped laughing. His victim's gasping breaths are slowing down – and then they stop completely. Then there's another chopping sound. It's that poor man's other hand, Hannah thinks. She's now holding onto Clay's hand as tightly as she can. Somehow, the warmth and strength of it comforts her.

to spurt	spritzen, schießen
to twitch	zucken
agony	(Höllen-)Qual
to comfort sb.	jmd. trösten
distorted	verzerrt
split second	Sekundenbruchteil
grim	grimmig, düster
to dance to sb.'s tune	nach jds. Pfeife tanzen

The screen goes black again and Hannah hopes it is over.
It isn't.

Now Hannah and the rest of the team hear heavy breathing coming from the monitor. It seems to fill the room. Somehow it frightens Hannah more than anything else. Until, that is, the killer finally speaks. His voice is distorted – but eerily quiet and calm.

"Dr Sheridan? Don't ever call Vidar a coward again. As you've just seen, he's not – I'm not. We'll speak again in the next few days. Oh, and Inspector McGowan? You seem very good at your job. And not bad to look at either; you should wear skirts more often. I'm really looking forward to talking with you, too – in person."

Exercise 29: Irregular verbs. Wie lauten Imperfekt und Partizip Perfekt der folgenden Verben?

1. ring _____ _____

2. fall _____ _____

3. take _____ _____

4. hold _____ _____

5. feel _____ _____

6. hit _____ _____

There is silence for a split second, then everything seems to happen at once. First, Chief Well's is suddenly back on the screen. His face looks grim. He gives the tablet to a constable while he talks quietly into his phone. When he's finished with the call, he tells the MIT that he's needed outside. Then the door to the incident room opens and Yolanda rushes back in. Two members of the Met's IT security team are with her.

"Is he still hacking into our conference?" she whispers.

"We don't know for sure," he whispers back. Then he seems to lose control.

"Enough!" he shouts and slams a fist down on the table.

"It's time for us to stop dancing to this killer's tune. As if it's not enough that he bombards us with his sick crimes and clues. Now he's even threatening two of our team members."

"Quinn!" Hannah interrupts him as she finally lets go of Clay's hand. "His threats aren't important right now, but the old man on the screen is! He looks familiar, though right now I can't say why. But most importantly, he could still be alive! We must try to find him. The killer might even still be at the scene – wherever it is."

her face falls	sie ist sichtlich enttäuscht
territory	Gebiet
furious	wütend, zornig
to bet	wetten
reluctantly	ungern, widerwillig
fuzzy	unklar, verschwommen

Hannah's face falls when she says this. It is true. They have no idea where this crime has taken place.

"I don't think so," Clay says and shakes his head. "What we just saw wasn't happening live. We can't know how long ago this attack happened. But it was at night – and in Oxford."

"How do you know that, Clay?" Quinn asks a little sceptically.

"Because of the bell in the background, Quinn. It kept on ringing and ringing until the screen went black. It must have been Great Tom ⓘ chiming in Oxford. I studied psychology there and I know Great Tom rings 101 times every night starting at 9:05 p.m."

"Good work, Clay." Quinn tells him. Then he turns to Yolanda.

"Inform the Thames Valley Police right away, Yolanda. Oxford is in their territory."

While Yolanda rushes out of the room again, Clay stands up, goes over to Quinn and speaks quietly into his ear.

Die **Great Tom** genannte Glocke ist die lauteste Glocke in Oxford. Die Tradition, diese Glocke jeden Abend um 21.05 Uhr genau 101 Mal zu läuten, stammt aus dem 17. Jahrhundert. Es gab einen Glockenschlag für jeden der ursprünglich 101 Studenten als Aufforderung, auf die Zimmer zu gehen, bevor die College Tore für die Nacht geschlossen wurden.

"So now it's certain that the killer is spying on us. Otherwise, he couldn't know about the VC and

58

interrupt it with such perfect timing. He even knows what Hannah is wearing!"

Exercise 30: Complete the definitions. Vervollständigen Sie die Definitionen mit der passenden Redewendung!

1. When you are disappointed, your _____ _____.

2. If someone else seems to be controlling your life, you feel as if you are _____ _____.

3. Something that happens very fast takes only a _____.

4. If you are hungry but don't have much time, then you quickly grab _____.

This thought frightens Clay and makes him furious. But he can't do anything about it right now – or can he?

"Quinn, I bet he's still watching. Let me talk to him again!"

"No, Clay. Not this time. If he's still there, let him see some real police work. I'm not letting you scare him away before Chief Well's people get a trace on him. Now sit back down!"

Clay nods reluctantly and Quinn turns to Hannah.

"You said before that the victim in Oxford looks familiar. I think I've seen him before, too. But the memory is fuzzy. Think hard, Hannah! Do you have any idea where you could have seen him?"

Hannah frowns while she tries to remember. "I think it has something to do with my parents. My mum's a solicitor and dad's a barrister.[1] When I was younger, I often watched dad at court."

"That's it, Hannah! I've got it now. The Oxford victim is a judge!"

"Kinkaid!" Hannah cries out. "Judge John Kinkaid. I'm pretty sure he retired several years ago."

Barrister und **solicitor** bezeichnen in Großbritannien zwei verschiedene Arten von Anwälten. Ein **solicitor** ist ein Anwalt, der seine Mandanten hauptsächlich außerhalb des Gerichts und in niedrigen Instanzen (z.B. vor einem Amtsgericht) vertritt. Ein **barrister** dagegen ist ein Spezialist für den Gerichtssaal.

Exercise 31: Verb forms. Lesen Sie weiter und ergänzen Sie die richtige Verbform!

"Excuse me, DCI Baxter?" The voice **1.** come _____ from the monitor. "Here is Constable Ed Jenkins. Did someone just **2.** say _____ the name John Kinkaid?"

"Yes," Quinn answers impatiently. "Why are you **3.** ask _____?"

"It's just, well, I **4.** hear _____ that name before."

"In what context, Constable?" Quinn asks.

"From my cousin, Sylvia," the constable replies. "She... um... she's often said quite awful things about him – and about our former Lord Mayor, too."

60

"What kind of things, Constable Jenkins?"

"Well, that they 'deserve what's coming to them' and 'killing is too good for them,' – things like that."

"And why would she say such things, Constable?" Quinn asks.

"It's a complicated story, sir. Oh hell! That reminds me, Sylvia has been trying to call me all morning."

"Constable Jenkins, you can give me the tablet back now."

Chief Wells has returned from outside.

"DCI Baxter? You were right! The surveillance team picked up a signal being sent from inside the crime scene. They couldn't trace it, though, and it's gone now. But they have a lead on the signal that interrupted our VC. It was coming from a council housing estate

court	Gericht
to deserve what's coming to one	kriegen, was man verdient
to pick up	*hier*: empfangen
council housing estate	Sozialwohnungs-anlage
resident	Bewohner, Anwohner
complaint	Klage, Beschwerde

in Central Sheffield. I'm sending patrol cars to the area, but it's a long shot. The Lansdowne Complex has three towers with over 150 flats."

"All you can do is try, Chief. Thanks."

"DCI Baxter, I've just learnt that something else strange is going on here. About 20 local residents contacted the police this morning with the same complaint. A courier delivered bizarre packets to their homes early this morning. One of them had a wedding ring inside it. And all of them contain what looks like human bones – and a cryptic note – from Vidar."

"What do the notes say, Chief?"

"Revenge is best served cold. Regards, Vidar."

Exercise 32: Word spiral. Welche Begriffe werden gesucht? Lösen Sie die Wortspirale!

1	2	3	4	5	6
20	21	22	23	24	7
19	32	33	34	25	8
18	31	36	35	26	9
17	30	29	28	27	10
16	15	14	13	12	11

1-4: above, higher or more than

4-12: the people who live in a building or area are its ...

12-20: someone who helps people with legal problems

20-28: If you don't really want to do something, you are ...

28-36: a region or area

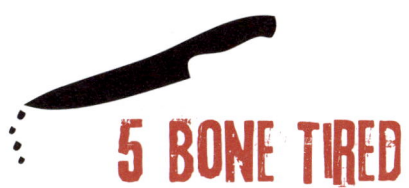

5 BONE TIRED

Vidar yawns sleepily in front of the telly in his home in central Sheffield. He's been awake for over 40 hours now and is exhausted. He'll allow himself to

to yawn	gähnen
crowd	Menschenmenge
bone tired	hundemüde
turntable	Plattenspieler

sleep for a while after the news. He takes a sip of tea and then turns up the volume on the television. The BBC is showing the 11 a.m. police news conference live. Vidar smiles when he sees the crowd of reporters outside New Scotland Yard. His smile widens when he sees DCI Baxter, Dr Sheridan and Inspector McGowan standing behind Police Commissioner Curtis Fletcher.

They all look grim – and bone tired, too, he thinks, congratulating himself on his choice of words. He can imagine that they are very tired of bones – but not as tired as they will be.

Vidar listens with interest as the Commissioner briefs the reporters and laughs when they start bombarding him with questions. It seems this is the first time they have heard about the murders of Neal Walsh and Judge Kinkaid.

Vidar is disappointed, though, when the Commissioner quickly ends the news conference. He didn't even mention my name, Vidar thinks angrily. That will change soon, he promises himself.

He switches off the telly and turns on an old-fashioned turntable. The sound of classical music fills the room. It's a solo-

63

piano version of his favourite song, the Brahms' Lullaby. The recording is old and scratched, but that doesn't bother Vidar. As always, the melody calms him.

On his way to bed, Vidar sings the words softly to himself. "Lullaby and goodnight, thy[i] mother's delight..."

Thy (dein) ist ein veralteter Begriff. Wie im Deutschen gab es im Englischen lange eine Unterscheidung zwischen „Sie" und „du". In der Alltagssprache überlebt hat nur die förmlichere Form **you**, die ursprünglich „Sie" bedeutete. Die Duz-Form **thou** begegnet einem nur noch selten.

Exercise 33: Synonyms. Finden Sie im vorherigen Textabschnitt die Wörter mit ähnlicher Bedeutung!

1. exhausted _____

2. furiously _____

3. to trouble _____

4. to update _____

5. very serious _____

6. telly _____

7. to assume _____

8. joy _____

Commissioner Fletcher looks anything but delighted. As soon as the news conference is finished, he turns to Quinn.

"Come with me. Now."

64

As they walk back into the building, he practically hisses at Quinn. "The reporters were already going crazy with MP Ashworth's murder, and now we have two more! I'm also getting pressure from high up to find and catch this killer. Even the Prime Minister has called!"

"We're working on it as hard as we can, Commissioner Fletcher."

"Work harder! Three respectable, well-known men have been brutally murdered in their homes. Find out who did it and why – before he can strike again."

What does he think we are doing? Quinn asks himself. He is glad when his mobile rings so he can escape the Commissioner's tongue-lashing.

lullaby	Wiegenlied
scratched	zerkratzt
ϟ from high up	von ganz oben
respectable	anständig, respektiert
ϟ tongue-lashing	Standpauke
firearms unit	bewaffnete Polizeieinheit
interrogation	Verhör, Befragung
to not take any chances	kein Risiko eingehen

"Excuse me, Commissioner. It's Chief Wells from Sheffield."

"DCI Baxter," Wells says excitedly when Quinn answers. "We've got a suspect! His name's Henry Lawton. He's the courier that delivered all of those packets this morning. And he lives in one of the towers in the Lansdowne Complex. It seems he also has a very good motive for the murders. I'll tell you the details later. I'm sending a firearms unit to bring him in for interrogation."

"A firearm's unit, Chief? Isn't that a bit unusual at this point?"

"Listen, Chief Inspector, it really looks like Lawton is the killer. I saw what he did to Neal – and to Judge Kinkaid. I'm not taking any chances of him using his axe on one of my officers!"

Quinn makes a split-second decision.

Exercise 34: Make it stronger! Lesen Sie weiter und setzen Sie die stärkeren Entsprechungen richtig ein!

rush   investigate   interrogate   order   obsessed
with

"Chief Wells? The killer is **1.** interested in _____

_____ DI McGowan and Dr Sheridan. Can they be there

when you **2.** question _____ the suspect?"

"Good idea, DCI Baxter, but **3.** tell _____ them

to **4.** be quick _____. While they're on the

way, they can go online to **5.** find out about _____

_____ the Sheffield toxic waste lawsuit from the

1980s. That's Lawton's motive!"

Henry Lawton wakes up to the sound of loud knocking on the door of his bed-sit. ⓘ Then he hears shouting.

"Open up, Mr Lawton! It's the police."

Oh bloody hell. This is my worst nightmare, he thinks as he gets out of bed in a daze.

"Just a minute, I'm coming," Lawton calls out.

His eyes move quickly around the room to make sure nothing incriminating is lying out in the open. Then he puts on jeans and a t-shirt and goes to the door. He looks through the peephole and is shocked by what he sees. At least ten police officers are outside his door. Most of them are pointing guns at it – at him. Henry is scared now.

"What, what do you want?" he asks nervously.

"Open the door, Mr Lawton. Now! Or we'll kick it down."

"Okay, okay. Calm down. I'm opening it."

As soon as he does, the police rush inside his home. Two officers grab him by the arms and push him up against the wall. Another one starts searching him.

toxic waste	Giftmüll
lawsuit	Klage, Rechtsstreit
in a daze	benebelt, benommen
incriminating	belastend, verfänglich
peephole	Guckloch
⚡ copper	Bulle
search warrant	Durchsuchungsbefehl

"Hey, stop that! Let me go!"

"He's clean," one of the officers calls through the open door.

A female detective comes inside. Henry hadn't seen her through the peephole. She looks too young and pretty to be a copper.

"Mr Lawton, I'm Detective Inspector Ivey Munro, South Yorkshire Police. Please come with us. We have some questions for you."

"I don't understand. What's going on here?" Henry asks angrily. "Are you arresting me?"

"No, Mr Lawton," Inspector Munro tells him softly. She smiles when she sees Henry's very high-tech computer equipment. "Not

Ein bed-sit (Abk. für "bedroom-sitting room") ist ein meist möbliertes Zimmer und eine in Großbritannien übliche, günstige Form von Mietwohnung. Jeder Mieter hat ein Einzelzimmer, oft mit kleiner Kochnische, und teilt sich das Bad mit anderen Mietern.

yet. But we do have a search warrant for your home."

"Wait a minute. I, I…"

Henry was going to say that he wants to call his solicitor. But his face falls when he remembers he doesn't have one anymore.

"I need a coat, and some socks and shoes," he says quietly.

Inspector Munro looks down at Henry's bare feet.

"What are you staring at, Inspector? So I'm missing a toe. That's not a crime, is it?"

"No, Mr Lawson, but cutting them off other people is! Now, will you come with us peacefully? Or do we need to use force?"

Henry nods his head in agreement, but he doesn't speak. He has the right to remain silent – and he does.

Exercise 35: Word order. Bringen Sie die Sätze in die richtige Reihenfolge!

1. when   the   suspect   police   asleep   was   arrived   the

   _____

2. a   not   weapon   is   Henry   carrying

   _____

3. warrant   attractive   the   has   a   copper   search

   _____

4. incriminating   Inspector   looking   Munro   evidence   for   is

   _____

Less than half an hour after the end of the news conference, Hannah and Clay are on their way to Sheffield. Clay is driving and Hannah is using her smartphone to research the toxic waste lawsuit. For a few minutes, Clay lets himself forget the reason for this trip. The weather is fine and he is enjoying the sunshine on his face. Clay loves travelling and he starts to imagine what it would be like to go on a real journey – with Hannah. He

bare	nackt, barfuß, bloß
force	*hier*: Gewalt, Zwang
journey	Reise
claim	Klage
birth defect	Geburtsfehler
complainant	Kläger
limbs *pl*	Gliedmaßen
to harm	schaden, verletzen

feels her eyes on him and turns his head and smiles at her. She smiles back and Clay suddenly wants to share his thoughts with her. But Hannah starts talking first – about the case.

"The lawsuit was about a claim that the City of Sheffield was responsible for a large increase in birth defects in the area, beginning in the late 1970s."

"Oh, of course. I was only 13 or 14 at the time, but I remember the photographs in the newspaper of some of the complainants. The defects were on their limbs, right?"

"Yes. There was a significant increase in the number of babies born in the area with missing or deformed fingers and toes. This started happening just months after the city began cleaning up the brownfield site of an old steel factory."

"Hannah, that could explain Vidar's motive – his 'bone-by-bone' plan, so to speak."

Eine **brownfield site** bezeichnet eine Industriebrache. In England gibt es ungefähr 63.750 Hektar solchen Brachlands.

"Yes!" Hannah's voice is excited now. "Vidar cuts off the hands and feet of the people he thinks harmed those children. Then he sends their bones to the people he believes are the real victims – the complainants in the lawsuit."

69

"Slow down, Hannah. We don't have the DNA analysis of the bones, yet. And were Vidar's victims even involved in the trial?" Hannah looks back down at her phone display.

"Well, Kinkaid was the judge who ruled against the complainants. And Neal Walsh and Malcolm Ashworth were both members of the Sheffield City Council back then.

Exercise 36: Translation. Lesen Sie weiter und übersetzen Sie die Verben. Achten Sie auf die richtige Zeitform!

"Yes, but the council 1. nicht erzeugen _____ the toxic waste – the old steel company 2. tun _____ that," Clay 3. erinnern _____ her.

"That's true, but the city 4. anheuern _____ a company to 5. säubern _____ the site."

"This company dug up the hazardous materials that the steel producers had buried in pits and transported the waste in open lorries," Hannah continues. "As a result, some of the waste spilt onto the roads and contaminated dust got into the air. Of course, people breathed this in, including pregnant women. The lawyers argued that the city had been negligent and was therefore liable for the birth defects."

"So Judge Kinkaid's ruling must have disappointed and angered a lot of people. Was Henry Lawton one of them?"

"I don't know, Clay. His name isn't mentioned in any of the online reports I've just seen. But that doesn't mean anything."

"No, it doesn't," Clay says thoughtfully.

"Clay? Do you mind if I close my eyes for a bit? That sometimes helps me think. And right now, I need to work out how this toxic waste case fits in with the killer profile you gave us this morning."

to rule against sb.	gegen jmd. entscheiden
City Council	Gemeinderat
hazardous	gefährlich
pit	Grube
to spill	verschütten
negligent	fahrlässig
liable	verantwortlich, haftbar
ruling	Urteil

"Yes, but I wrote that last night before I had learned about the Walsh and Kinkaid murders or the Sheffield police had come up with their suspect. And before he threatened you – us."

"Oh you're not taking that seriously, are you?"

"Yes, Hannah, I am. As I've said before, this killer has a reason for everything. It worries me that he's got his eye on you, too."

Exercise 37: Checking the facts. Ordnen Sie die Satzteile richtig zu!

1. ☐ Judge Kinkaid ruled   **a)** transported in open lorries.

2. ☐ The killer has threatened   **b)** the city was liable.

3. ☐ Hazardous waste was   **c)** against the complainants.

4. ☐ The complainants believed   **d)** Clay and Hannah.

headquarters	Zentrale, Hauptquartier
one-way glass	Spiegelglas
to single sb. out	jmd. auswählen
Ask away.	Fragen Sie nur!
numerous	zahlreich
on sick leave	krankgeschrieben
business on the side	Nebengeschäft
recipient	Empfänger

"So he's not talking?" Hannah asks Chief Wells and Detective Inspector Munro.

Hannah and Clay have just arrived at Carbrook House, the new headquarters for the South Yorkshire Police in Sheffield.

"No," the Inspector answers. "He refused to say a word until he spoke with a lawyer. One arrived ten minutes ago. That's him sitting in there with Lawton now."

Hannah looks through the one-way glass that separates the interrogation room from the room next door where the police are. "The one in the grey suit is the lawyer, of course. The other one is Lawton," Chief Wells adds.

Henry Lawton is quite tall and muscular and in his early 50s. He's also very good-looking, Hannah thinks.

"They almost never look like monsters, do they?" Clay says grimly. It's as if he's reading her mind.

"Doctor? Inspector? We think that since the killer has singled you out, you should wait here for now. We'll bring you into the questioning at a later point. Let's surprise *him* for a change."

Hannah and Clay agree and Chief Wells and Inspector Munro go inside and sit down across from Lawton and the solicitor, John Dunn. Then the DI turns on the recording device. It's 3 p.m.

"Mr Lawton, do you understand why you are here?" she asks.

"No, I don't. You've made a terrible mistake. I'm not a killer!"

"I didn't say that, sir."

"No, but that's what you think. Mr Dunn told me you believe I'm involved in those axe murders I heard about on TV."

72

"We just have some questions," Chief Wells says calmly. "Will you answer them now?"

Henry looks at the solicitor and John Dunn nods for yes.

"Ask away. I don't have anything to hide."

Exercise 38: Nouns. Lesen Sie weiter und ergänzen Sie die fehlenden Substantive!

"Fine, Mr Lawton," DI Munro says. "Numerous **1.** *f* _____ in the Sheffield **2.** *a* _____ received strange **3.** *p* _____ at their **4.** *h* _____ early this morning. And all of them have identified you as the **5.** *c* _____. But your **6.** *b* _____ told us you've been on sick leave for the past month. So what were you doing working, and where did those packages come from?"

"I, I have, well a little business on the side. Sometimes I make, um, special deliveries. I was contacted through my homepage about doing the ones today. The client offered me double my usual rate if I could deliver everything before 9 a.m. today."

"And where did you pick up the packages?"

"I didn't. He brought them to me around five this morning."

"And what did this mysterious 'client' of yours look like?"

"I didn't really get a good look at him. Tall, though. Like me."

"And do you know any of the package recipients?"

"Sort of. They were all involved in the lawsuit."

73

⚡ bugger	*hier*: Arschloch
stunned	fassungslos
curtly	barsch
to intervene	eingreifen
to ID sb.	jmd. identifizieren

"Do you mean the toxic waste lawsuit against the city of Sheffield? The one your own two daughters were also involved in? The one that Judge John Kinkaid ruled against?"

"That old **bugger**? He got what he deserved. But it wasn't me that did him in!" he added quickly.

Just then Constable Jenkins knocks on the door and comes in. He gives Chief Wells a plastic bag and whispers something to him that makes him smile.

"Well maybe you can explain this, Mr Lawton!"

Chief Wells puts the plastic evidence bag on the table. There's an American passport inside.

"We just found this fake US passport taped beneath your lorry. The name on it is David Smith – but the photo inside is yours."

Henry is **stunned** and stares helplessly at the lawyer.

John Dunn sees the panic in Henry's eyes and stands up.

"Chief, Inspector, I'd like to speak with Mr Lawton again. Alone."

Chief Wells tells DI Munro to call him when the questioning can restart. Then the DI and Constable Jenkins join Hannah and Clay.

"Did you see the look on Lawton's face when he saw the passport?" Inspector Munro tells them proudly. "But it's his own fault. How stupid of him to hide it under his lorry."

"How do you know that it belongs to him – or that he hid it under his own vehicle?" Hannah asks. "Are his fingerprints on it?"

"No. Actually, there aren't any prints on it at all."

"And what about the tape? Any prints there?"

"No. So he was wearing gloves," the Inspector answers **curtly**. Then she smiles sweetly over at Clay. "Dr Sheridan, it seems

74

Inspector McGowan doubts that Lawton is our man. What's your opinion?"

"I think it's too soon to say, Inspector. And please, call me Clay."

"Why thank you, Clay. And my name's Ivey."

Exercise 39: Reported speech. DI Munro berichtet was der Verdächtige sagte. Wandeln Sie die Sätze in Indirekte Rede um!

1. "The employer reports that Lawton has been on sick leave."

   _____

2. "The suspect says he has a job on the side."

   _____

3. "Lawton admits that he knows some of the families."

   _____

4. "Lawton claims he was contacted through his homepage."

   _____

To Hannah, it seems they are flirting. She's surprised to realize she doesn't like this idea and decides to intervene.

"And I'm Hannah. Look Ivey, it's not that I have doubts. I just agree with Clay that it's too early to say for sure. Why not send a copy of the passport to our MIT in London? They can show the photo to the hotel receptionist and see if she can ID Lawton."

75

Two can play at that game.	Wie du mir, so ich dir.
to devastate	zerstören, umhauen
to blame sb.	jmd. die Schuld geben
to divorce sb.	sich von jmd. scheiden lassen

"Brilliant idea, Hannah," Clay says, but Hannah ignores him.

"And we should also have a voice analysis done. I couldn't tell if Lawton's voice is the same as the distorted one we heard during the VC, but maybe our computer experts can."

"Okay, Hannah. Those are good ways to help us prove that Lawton is the killer. I'll start the ball rolling."

"And I'd like to learn more about the toxic waste case – and Lawton's role in it," Clay adds.

"I think I can tell you about that, Dr Sheridan," Constable Jenkins offers. "My cousin Sylvia was also involved. But like I said this morning, it's a long story."

"Well, we have time now Constable Jenkins," Hannah says and gives him one of her sexiest smiles. "Or may I call you Ed?"

Two can play at that game, she thinks.

"Why, of course, Inspector."

"It's Hannah, Ed. While Clay was driving us here, I did some research on the case. How is Henry Lawton involved in it?"

"Henry Lawton's wife had twin daughters with much more serious defects. They were also complainants in the lawsuit."

"But Ed, why did Judge Kinkaid rule against the complainants? From what I've read, their case seemed very strong."

"Well, in his ruling the judge said that the complainants hadn't proven that the toxic waste caused the birth defects. Judge Kinkaid pointed out that the twin's father was born missing a toe. In the judge's opinion, the defects were genetic."

"That must have devastated Henry Lawton."

76

"It did, Hannah – and his wife blamed [i] the lawsuit loss on Henry. After the decision, she divorced him, took the girls and left."

That reminds Clay of something. "Did the twins also receive packets with bones today?"

Vorsicht, falsche Freunde:	
to blame sb.	≠ jmd. blamieren
to blame sb.	jmd. die Schuld geben
to embarrass sb. (in public)	jmd. blamieren

"No, they didn't. They couldn't. The Lawton twins are dead."

Exercise 40: Unscramble. Bilden Sie sinnvolle Wörter aus dem Buchstabensalat und finden Sie das Lösungswort!

1. gintlegen ⁀⁀⁀☐⁀⁀⁀⁀⁀⁀

2. lutaf ⁀☐⁀⁀⁀

3. elyarw ⁀⁀☐⁀⁀⁀

4. xtico seawt ⁀⁀⁀⁀⁀⁀⁀☐⁀

5. llrnugi ⁀☐⁀⁀⁀⁀

6. wfodrnbile ⁀⁀⁀⁀☐⁀⁀⁀

7. stniw ☐⁀⁀⁀⁀

Lösung: ☐☐☐☐☐☐☐

77

6 HARD WORK – AND PLAY

"The twins committed suicide about 15 years ago," Ivey explains to Hannah and Clay. "They had just turned 16. Everyone says they were beautiful girls, except for..."

"Their webbed fingers and toes," Ed says sadly.

"Yes, but why would Lawton wait so long to act?" Clay adds thoughtfully. "And why would he only target two former members of the Sheffield City Council?"

"A lot of the former council members were already quite elderly at the time. So I imagine that many of them have since died – of natural causes," Ivey says. "But I'll check it."

"Ivey?" Hannah interrupts. "You should also warn any of them that are still alive to be extra careful. Just in case..."

"Of course, Hannah, but I know how to do my job! Now, Clay,

to commit suicide	Selbstmord begehen
webbed	mit Schwimm-häuten, ver-wachsen
to target	*hier*: ins Visier nehmen
frantically	verzweifelt
to confirm	bestätigen

to your first question, who knows what makes a killer tick?"

"Clay does, Ivey," Hannah says sweetly. "That's his job."

Ivey gives Hannah a nasty look. "Yes, of course, I didn't mean..."

"Um, Inspector Munro?" Constable Jenkins interrupts. "I think the duty solicitor needs our help. Look."

78

Exercise 41: Prepositions. Lesen Sie weiter und setzen Sie die Präpositionen richtig ein!

out   to   through   with   up   at

All four of them stare **1.** _____ the one-way glass.

John Dunn is waving **2.** _____ them **frantically**

3. _____ one hand and using the other one

4. _____ hold Henry Lawton's head **5.** _____ .

Blood is pouring **6.** _____ of the suspect's nose.

"The coroner in Oxford confirms that Judge Kinkaid died last night," Quinn tells the rest of the MIT members in London.

They are having a late afternoon meeting in the incident room.

"That means we have three dead men in three different locations in less than 24 hours. The timing bothers me. Doreen, have you finished the computer simulation I asked for?" Quinn asks the HOLMES 2 expert.

"Yes, Quinn. If Lawton is the killer, he would have had time to commit the Ashworth murder, travel to Sheffield and kill Walsh, and then go on to Oxford for his third victim last night."

"Yes, but the killer's work didn't end with the murders. He had to go somewhere to remove the flesh from his victim's bones. Dr Tong is analysing them now, but he says it looks as if he boiled them. That must have been a very smelly business. Then the killer had to pack the bones and notes, deliver the parcels in Sheffield and do that in time to 'be' at our VC this morning."

79

Doreen looks at the printout in front of her.

"Theoretically, Lawton had enough time for all of that. But it's a very tight schedule, and only possible if he travelled by vehicle. No combination of public transportation would have worked."

"And only possible if nothing went wrong or got in the way."

"Yes. A ten-minute traffic jam would have ruined the whole plan."

"Hmm. That doesn't really fit in with Clay's profile of a careful planner, does it? Doreen, send your report to Clay and Hannah. Then start comparing images from the CCTV cameras closest to the crime scenes in London, Sheffield and Oxford."

"You want me to find his vehicle, Quinn?" Doreen asks in a tired voice. "That could take hours – even days."

"Well Doreen, like they say, hard work never killed anyone."

Exercise 42: Timeline. Bringen Sie die Schritte des Täters in die richtige Reihenfolge!

a) Break into the police video conference.

b) Murder Judge Kinkaid.

c) Install cameras in the Ashworth townhouse.

d) Cook the bones.

e) Drive from London to the Walsh cottage in Sheffield.

1	2	3	4	5

"He'll be fine," Ivey tells Clay and Hannah. "Lawton told the doctor we called that he gets nosebleeds when he's over excited. In my opinion, it's just one more sign of his guilt."

80

Clay and Hannah don't comment on this, but Clay has a feeling in his bones that nosebleeds and Vidar just don't go together.

"Anyway, we can't talk to Lawton anymore today. Doctor's orders. So will you two go back to London now? Or would you prefer to stay here overnight?" Ivey asks and

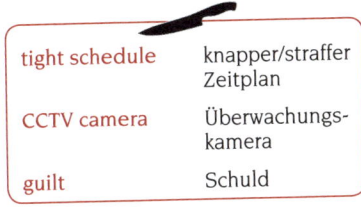

tight schedule	knapper/straffer Zeitplan
CCTV camera	Überwachungs-kamera
guilt	Schuld

gives Clay another one of her flirty smiles.

But it's Hannah who answers Ivey's question. "I checked in with our DCI in London while you were busy, Ivey. He wants us to stay and continue our work here. If that's okay with you and Chief Wells, of course."

Exercise 43: Confusing words? Lesen Sie weiter und unterstreichen Sie die richtige Variante!

"No problem. Do you 1. want / like me to recommend 2. accommodations / accomodation ?"

"Thanks, but our officer manager has already 3. done / made reservations for us at The Brewery Hotel."

"Oh, lucky you! It has a very fine 4. sight / view of the River Don. And they brew 5. their / there own beer. It would be a great place to meet 6. us / each other later. I've got a meeting with the Chief and the team now, but after that, we can celebrate the fact that we've 7. caught / catched the killer."

splendid	großartig, ausgezeichnet
to beam	strahlen
ale	obergäriges Bier
⚡ to dig in	reinhauen, es sich schmecken lassen
Yorkshire Pudding	traditionelle Beilage aus Teig zum Roast Beef
low-cut	(tief) dekolletiert

"But we don't...," Hannah starts to say when Clay interrupts her.

"That's a splendid idea, Ivey. Ed? Why don't you come, too. And invite Chief Wells and the other members of your team."

Hannah has had just about enough of whatever is going on between Ivey and Clay. But she covers it up by trying to sound very professional.

"Wonderful. Then let's get back to work now. Clay would really like to see the Neal Walsh murder scene in person, Ivey. And Ed? I want to speak to your cousin, Sylvia. Can you arrange that?"

"Sure, Hannah. I'll call her – and I'll ask the Chief if I can miss the meeting and take you there, too. I'll also be glad to drive you to the hotel afterwards."

"Cheers,[1] Ed," Hannah says with a big smile.

Im British English bedeutet **Cheers** nicht nur „Prost!" beim Anstoßen. Man benutzt es auch im Sinne von „danke!" oder auch wie „Tschüss", z.B. auch in E-Mails oder informellen Briefen.

Constable Jenkins beams back at her, and suddenly Hannah isn't the only one who's jealous.

At 7:30 that evening, Hannah and Clay are sitting with a group of Sheffield police officers in the lively pub of The Brewery Hotel. The waiter has just brought them another round of ale and their starters. Everyone raises their glasses, says "cheers" and digs in.

82

Exercise 44: Adjectives and adverbs. Lesen Sie weiter und setzen Sie die richtige Wortform ein!

fine   tight   polite   delicious   real

"This is **1.** _____ tasty," Ed says after he tries his Yorkshire Pudding. "Do you want some? It's **2.** _____.

"No thanks, Ed. I'm **3.** _____ with my salad," she tells him **5.** _____ just as Ivey arrives.

The DI is wearing a low-cut sweater and **5.** _____ jeans.

Too tight, Hannah thinks.

"I'm sorry I'm late, everyone," Ivey says as she sits down next to Clay. "I was waiting for our IT experts' first report about Lawton's computer equipment."

"Did they find anything incriminating?" Chief Wells asks.

"No, not really." Ivey stops talking. The waiter has come over to take her order.

When he leaves, she continues. "There are lots of files about the toxic waste lawsuit on it. But his internet usage chronology is empty and there were no files with videos or photos from the crime scenes on it."

"Maybe he's got a laptop hidden somewhere else," Ed suggests.

"We need to check that tomorrow, Ivey," Chief Wells says and takes another sip of his ale. Then he turns to Clay.

"So, Dr Sheridan, was your visit to the crime scene helpful? I'm interested in hearing what you were hoping to find."

Clay sighs. He hates questions like this. It's hard to explain exactly what he does at a crime scene. Most people, even police officers, don't understand.

passionate	leidenschaftlich
intention	Absicht, Vorhaben
to be caught red-handed	auf frischer Tat ertappt werden
in advance	im Voraus
saw dust	Sägemehl
insightful	aufschlussreich
to purr	schnurren
to have a clean record	nicht vorbestraft sein

"Yes, Chief. Visiting a crime scene is always important in my work. I won't go into all the details, but for example, being there confirmed some of my theories about the killer."

"Such as?" Ivey asks and leans in a little closer to him.

"He's an extremely careful planner. He's very, well, passionate about what he does. But he doesn't take any chances. He has no intention of being caught red-handed. It's also part of his system to visit his crime scenes in advance. At least, he did that at the Ashworth and Walsh homes. I don't know yet about Oxford, but it seems likely."

"How can you be sure about the advance visits?"

"The cameras. We have his recording of the Ashworth murder, and it starts with MP Ashworth going to the front door. In the Walsh case, there was a lot of saw dust on the two cameras your team found in the workshop. So he must have installed them at some earlier point."

"Yes, but we police officers don't need a profiler to tell us that."

"This morning, Clay gave our MIT a list of questions he came up with from the Ashworth crime scene that are very insightful," Hannah says. "We just haven't had time to answer them, yet."

"Can you show them to us, too, Clay?"

Ivey is practically purring now, and it makes Hannah feel a little sick. She puts down her fork and pushes the rest of her salad away as Clay smiles at Ivey.

"Okay Ivey, why not? There are a lot of experienced officers at the table." Clay reaches into his briefcase. "Here's my copy with some notes I added this afternoon."

Exercise 45: Question words. **Lesen Sie weiter und vervollständigen Sie Clays Notizen mit dem entsprechenden Fragewort!**

1. _____ did perp pre-visit houses?
   (No break-in reports!)

2. _____ did MP let perp inside?

3. _____ do removed trousers mean?
   (not Walsh's or Kinkaid's!)

4. _____ tying dead MP to piano sym-
   bolic?

5. _____ picture was in the frame?
   (Ask E.A) *Lawton's twins?*

"Those are all interesting points, Dr Sheridan," Chief Wells says. "Now I have a question for you: What do your profiler instincts tell you – is Henry Lawton our man? As far as we know, Lawton has a clean record."

"Maybe," Clay says tactfully. "I need to talk to him myself. And we should have the voice analysis tomorrow, anyway."

In that moment, the waiter brings Ivey's drink and starter.

"Your main courses will be here soon," the waiter says as he starts clearing away glasses, plates and cutlery. "Does anyone need anything else right now?"

"I'll have another ale," Hannah tells him.

"I think we all will," the Chief adds. "And this round's on me."

"Hannah, did you learn anything from Sylvia Tidwell?" Clay asks after he finally takes a sip of his beer.

"Why yes, Clay. Thanks for finally asking. Mrs Tidwell gave me a lot of background information about the lawsuit. And sorry Ed, but she's a bit of a gossip. She had quite a lot to say about Henry Lawton, too."

"Like what?"

Exercise 46: Correct the mistakes. Lesen Sie weiter und korrigieren Sie die sechs Fehler im folgenden Absatz!

"Mrs Tidwell told that Lawton use to be very outgoing. But since his daughters killed themself, he stops going out. She also means he has money problem."

1. _____   2. _____

3. _____   4. _____

5. _____   6. _____

86

Hannah takes a sip of her ale. "But the most important thing I learned wasn't about Lawton."

"And what was that, Hannah?" Ivey interrupts.

She doesn't like the way Clay is looking at his colleague with such interest.

"She may have given us a clue as to why the murderer targeted MP Ashworth and Neal Walsh."

Hannah stops for a moment to enjoy the looks on everyone's faces – especially Clay's.

cutlery	Besteck
This round's on me!	Diese Runde geht auf mich!
outgoing	aufgeschlossen
to soothe	beruhigen
gulp	großer Schluck

"The two victims were very close friends with the owner of the company that was hired to clean up the Brownfield site. Landon Mead."

"Wait a minute!" Clay exclaims. "Isn't he married to one of the Ashworth party guests? The one who told us..."

"Yes, he is," Hannah cuts Clay off before he can say anything indiscreet about the dead MP.

The Sheffield police don't need to know about *that* – at least not now, she thinks.

"And after I finished talking to Sylvia, I called Sarah Mead. I wanted to, well, just check that everything is fine with her husband. He wasn't at the party. And I thought that if the toxic waste lawsuit really is the killer's motive, then Mr Mead would be a logical target for Vidar."

"And could she soothe your worried mind, Hannah?" Ivey asks curtly and finishes the whisky she's drinking in one gulp. Then she motions to the waiter to bring her another one.

"Yes, Ivey. Thank you, she did. It seems Mrs Mead and her husband don't call each other very often when he's away on business. I got the impression that the two of them don't have the best of marriages."

"Will she try and reach him?" Clay asks.

"She said she would call him tonight," Hannah replies, taking another sip of beer. "She has my mobile number and will text me after she's spoken to him."

"Well done, Hannah," Ivey says a little sarcastically. "It's good to know that Scotland Yard is so careful. But I don't think you need to worry about Mr Mead – or any other potential victims. I'm convinced that Vidar *is* Henry Lawton – and he's safely locked up in jail tonight. So why don't we all relax now and enjoy the rest of the evening?"

Exercise 47: Eating out. Finden Sie im Gitternetz 12 Begriffe rund ums Essengehen!

A	S	D	S	M	E	C	I	D	M
W	A	I	T	E	R	H	S	I	A
S	A	L	A	D	F	E	R	M	C
O	T	V	R	N	C	E	N	E	X
R	E	S	T	A	U	R	A	N	T
D	Q	U	E	X	T	S	L	U	P
E	M	R	R	G	L	H	E	E	U
R	D	K	O	J	E	N	O	B	B
I	S	E	W	D	R	I	N	K	S
W	H	I	S	K	Y	A	U	G	O

But Landon Mead isn't safe, and hasn't been for days.

Is it four or is it five days now? How long have I actually been in this damp, windowless room, he wonders. But it's not a room – it's my cell. How I hate it – especially that naked light bulb hanging from the ceiling. It's always on and I can't reach the switch to turn it off.

Angrily, he rattles the chain attached tightly to the metal cuff

convinced	überzeugt
damp	feucht
cuff	Handschelle
leaky	undicht, leck

around his right hand. The other end is fastened to a heavy iron ring on the wall. It's just above the mattress on the floor where Landon is sitting.

My God, this mattress stinks! But not as much as the leaky toilet does. At least there is one, even though it's hard to reach.

Landon looks down at his bare feet. They're chained together so closely that he can barely walk at all.

I'm getting good at hopping, though, he thinks, and makes a sound that is almost a laugh before he starts to cry – again.

No, I won't cry! I won't give him that satisfaction. But he's not here, is he? When did I see him last? And that thought starts the chain of questions that keep circling round and round in Landon's head. Where am I? What does he want? Is anybody looking for me? Does Sarah miss me?

No, of course not. And why should

Phrasal Verbs wie to put through haben oft mehrere Bedeutungen:

to put sb. through sth.	jmd. etw. durchmachen lassen
to put (sb.) through	jmd. verbinden, durchstellen
to put through (a deal)	ein Geschäft abschließen

she? But I'm not going to think about Sarah and all that I've put her through. **ⓘ** Not now. He starts to cry again.

"Stop it, Mead! Get a hold of yourself!"

I'm shouting, Landon suddenly realizes. I never shout. But it doesn't matter. No one can hear me. Unless... unless *he's* secretly listening – or watching me. Landon shivers. Which is worse? The few times the man was here... or the fact that I haven't seen him for... for a long time now. Not since he brought more bottled water. I'm sure it's drugged. But I have to drink, otherwise I'll die of thirst.

Landon suddenly has a horrible feeling. Is that it? Is that his plan? Is he going to leave me here to die? Alone? Like this? I don't deserve this!

Get a hold of yourself!	Reiß dich zusammen!
pinkie	kleiner Finger
slurred	undeutlich
to call it a night	Feierabend machen
to insist on	bestehen auf
unsteady	unsicher, wackelig
drained	erschöpft, erledigt

Without thinking, Landon slams his right hand down on the mattress – and then screams out in agony. When the pain finally fades again, the stumps where his thumb and pinkie used to be are bleeding again. He reluctantly takes a sip of water to try and calm himself.

Yes, it's *much* worse when Vidar is here.

At the pub, it's already after 11 p.m. Chief Wells signals the waiter and asks for the bill. His voice is a little bit slurred.

"All right everyone, time for us to call it a night – and if you've come by car, a taxi. We've all got a lot of work to do tomorrow."

Hannah stands up to thank the Chief – he's insisted on paying for everything. Clay sees that Hannah is a little unsteady on her feet. He gets up, too, and takes her arm.

Exercise 48: Translation. Lesen Sie weiter, übersetzen Sie die angegebenen Begriffe und setzen Sie sie richtig ein!

teilen zumindest merken endlich zustimmen

kennenlernen

When Ivey **1.** _____ this, she **2.** _____

accepts that she won't be **3.** _____ the profiler

better – **4.** _____ not tonight. She thankfully

5. _____ to **6.** _____ a taxi with Ed.

After all the Sheffield police have gone, Hannah suddenly sits down again. She suddenly feels completely drained. She remembers that she still hasn't received a message from Sarah Mead, but she pushes the thought of work away. That's not what's on her mind right now.

"Hannah? Is everything okay?" Clay asks and sits down next to her. Hannah doesn't answer at first.

Then she makes a decision. "I think I want to have a nightcap up in my room. Will you join me, Clay?"

Clay knows he shouldn't. In fact the words "don't do it, Sheridan, don't do it!" are ringing madly in his head. He ignores them.

"I guess one more drink won't hurt, will it?"

"No, it won't. But Clay, to be honest, I've had enough to drink. What I need right now is…," Hannah stops talking and looks quickly around the room just to make sure none of the Sheffield police have come back inside.

"This." Then she leans over and puts her lips on his.

7 GRISLY MESSAGES

The sound of the alarm on Clay's smartphone wakes him at 7:00 the next morning. Instinctively, he turns over to look at Hannah. She's already awake and staring dreamily up at the ceiling. When she senses his gaze, she turns towards him and smiles at him.

gaze	Blick
desirable	begehrenswert
to murmur	murmeln
to put business before pleasure	erst die Arbeit und dann das Vergnügen
tender	zärtlich

The sight makes Clay catch his breath. What's left of Hannah's make-up is a bit smeared and her curly brown hair is a little wild, but for Clay, this makes her even more beautiful – and desirable.

"Good morning, Hannah," he says and leans over to kiss her.

"Mm, morning to you too, Clay," she murmurs against his lips. Then she sighs and sits up. There isn't time for more right now.

"Hannah, um, should we talk about last night?"

Before she answers, Hannah pushes back the covers and gets out of bed. Her naked, curvy body is a breath-taking sight.

"Dr Sheridan, I know you psychologists always want to talk about everything, but I don't want to – at least not now. We have to put business before pleasure."

Hannah leans down and gives him a quick but tender kiss. Clay enjoys watching as Hannah starts picking up her clothes and

92

looking for her phone in her handbag. He frowns, though, when he sees the look on her face as she checks her phone for messages.

"So Mrs Mead still hasn't contacted you?"

"No," Hannah tells him as she goes towards the bathroom. "I'll call her as soon as I've finished getting dressed. But here's a message from Yolanda. She's set up another VC between the MIT and the police here in Sheffield. That means we need to hurry."

Exercise 49: Clay's appearance. Unterstreichen Sie die richtige Variante!

1. Clay's hairs are / hair is dark red with a few / a little grey.
2. His eyes are faint / pale blue and he wears a wire-framed glass / wire-framed glasses .
3. He's long / tall and weighs / weight just over 12 stone. [i]

Hannah and Clay arrive at the Sheffield police headquarters just before eight. Ed Jenkins is waiting for them and brings them to a small conference room. The only empty seats left are the ones next to Ivey.

"Sorry about yesterday, Hannah...," Ivey starts to apologize.

Der **stone** (1 stone = 6,35 kg) ist eine alte Maßeinheit. Dieses Maß wird für geschäftliche Zwecke nicht mehr benutzt, aber im britischen Sprachraum ist es immer noch üblich, Menschen in 'stones' und 'pounds' (1 stone = 14 pounds) zu wiegen.

to turn sth. over to sb.	etw. übergeben an jmd. anderen
to settle down	sich beruhigen
mug	Becher, Tasse
to bear sth.	etw. ertragen

But Chief Wells begins the meeting before she can finish.

"Good morning, everyone. I hope you all got a good night's sleep and are ready to get back to work."

Hannah and Clay share a smile at the chief's words.

"As you know, we're doing another VC with the MIT in London. I hope it won't be as dramatic as the one yesterday."

The MIT suddenly appears on the conference room screen and Chief Wells and Quinn greet each other. Then the Chief turns the meeting over to DCI Baxter.

"We have a lot to do, so I'll just get right to it. To start, an hour ago we received the first results of the DNA tests on the finger and toe bones sent to the families in Sheffield. As we suspected, they are from the three murder victims. However, bones from two of the fingers sent to Kevin Tidwell have, um, different origins..."

"What?" Clay exclaims loudly. He's not the only one who's shocked at this news.

"Yes, it's true," Quinn continues. "The pathologist says the bones from one pinkie and one thumb are NOT from MP Ashworth, Neal Walsh or Judge Kinkaid. Further, the thumb bones almost certainly came from a woman – and have yellowed with age. That means they were most likely removed some years ago. The pinkie bones are from a male."

The VC participants all start talking at once.

"Listen up, everyone," Quinn barks. "I've already got someone investigating those particular bones in more detail. And Doreen, get your computer people to cross-check this new information with HOLMES. Now, settle down everybody and let me continue."

94

At her home in London, Sarah Mead is trying not to give in to panic. She picks up her coffee mug, but her hands are shaking so badly she spills some down the front of her blouse. In a daze, she watches as the brown stain spreads across the pale-pink silk. She puts the mug down and looks at her gold watch. It's almost 8:30. She has to leave for her bank soon.

Exercise 50: Mixed tenses. Lesen Sie weiter und setzen Sie die Verben in der richtigen Zeitform ein!

read   pick up   look at   not believe   arrive

Nervously, she 1. _____ the open package on the table in front of her. It 2. _____ with the early morning post, and since then Sarah 3. _____ the letter inside it at least a dozen times. She still 4. _____ what it says, so she 5. _____ the letter and begins reading it once more.

Dear Mrs Mead,
Follow my instructions exactly – especially the ones concerning your bank account! If you do, I will not harm you, your sons or your grandchildren. If you don't...

Sarah blinks tears out of her eyes and looks at the package. But she can't bear to see – or touch – what's inside it again.

95

"Oh Landon!" she cries out helplessly. "Where are you?"
The letter falls slowly to the carpeted floor as Sarah buries her head in her hands.

"Now," Quinn continues, "I want to **move on** to another surprising development. Early last evening, The Bank of England let our financial investigators **review** MP Ashworth's bank **records** from his three accounts. Two of them are completely empty!"

"So the MP couldn't manage his money?" Ivey says. "That's nothing new for a politician; they're always **wasting** money – usually ours."

to move on	*hier*: weitermachen
to review	überprüfen
record	*hier*: Unterlagen
to waste	verschwenden
to transfer	überweisen

"The problem is," Quinn says firmly, "the accounts were emptied *after* the MP was dead. Whoever did it **transferred** the money with online banking. That means they had access to all the MP's bank details, including his TAN. And unfortunately, MP Ashworth didn't have a limit on how much he could transfer from his account every day."
"How much did they take?" Hannah asks.
"A lot. On the Saturday Ashworth turned 60, he had over 600,000 pounds in one account and almost a million in the other."
Once again, both groups of police start speculating at once.
"Maybe the wife *is* involved..."
"Or the housekeeper. Did we even check her alibi?"
"What about one of the MP's lovers?" Ivey asks.
Trust her to think of *that* aspect, Hannah thinks.
"Ivey, our own financial people need to check Neal's bank accounts, too," Chief Wells says. "And let our colleagues in Oxford

96

know about this new angle so they can look into Judge Kinkaid's finances."

Exercise 51: Word families. Ergänzen Sie die zu den Adjektiven gehörenden Substantive und Verben!

1. instructive _____ _____
2. accessible _____ _____
3. financial _____ _____
4. investigative _____ _____

"Quinn, where did the money go?" Hannah asks.

"Most of it went to different off-shore accounts in the Bahamas. Our money people are trying to trace it, but it won't be easy."

"You said 'most' of the money. What about the rest?"

"Yes, well 20,000 pounds went to a British bank account – in Sheffield. The account holder is Henry Lawton."

Then let's see what he has to say about it!" Hannah says excitedly. "Chief Wells? I think it's time for you to let me and Clay interview Mr Lawton!"

But Clay is shaking his head. "I just can't see 'Vidar' sending money to his own bank account. He's far too clever for that. It must be some kind of trick – the real killer is playing games with us again."

"Or that's just what Harry Lawton wants us to think," Ivey replies. "But Hannah's right. Let's ask him!"

Just then a young constable comes in. "Excuse me, Chief. But this parcel just came for Dr Sheridan. It's marked 'urgent' and it

regulations *pl*	Vorschriften, Bestimmungen
⚡ Bloody hell!	Ach du Scheiße!
knuckle	Fingerknöchel
to jump to conclusions	voreilige Schlüsse ziehen
accomplice	Komplize
engraving	Gravierung
on the double	sofort, im Eiltempo
to tremble	beben, zittern

looks exactly like the ones all the families received yesterday, so I thought…"

"You thought right, Constable Walker. Give it to Dr Sheridan."

"Clay, wait!" Hannah warns. "It could be a bomb!"

"Don't worry, Inspector," Chief Wells tells her. "It's standard procedure here to inspect all mail for explosive devices. Constable Walker, you did follow the regulations?"

"Of course, sir!"

"Here, Clay, put on these first," Hannah says and gives him a pair of latex gloves she's taken out of her bag.

Everyone holds their breath as the profiler puts on the gloves and opens the package. His face turns pale when he sees what's inside. Hannah and Ivey can see it, too.

"Bloody! Hell!" Ivey exclaims and Hannah couldn't agree with her more.

"What is it, Dr Sheridan?" Chief Wells cries out.

Obwohl **tweezers** (Pinzette) ein Einzelobjekt ist, wird es wie ein Pluralbegriff behandelt, weil es zwei identische Hälften hat. Andere solcher „Paarwörter" sind z.B. *scissors, trousers* und *glasses*. Z.B. *These trousers **are** too small.*

"Is it more bones, Clay?" Quinn asks impatiently.

"Not exactly," Clay answers softly. "Does anyone have a pair of tweezers ❶?"

Ivey quickly searches in her bag until she finds a pair and silently hands them to Clay.

Exercise 52: Prepositions. Lesen Sie weiter und ergänzen Sie die fehlenden Präpositionen!

At first, everyone **1.** _____ both rooms can only stare **2.** _____ what Clay then holds **3.** _____ with the tweezers. It's an entire bloody finger – **4.** _____ a gold ring stuck **5.** _____ top of the knuckle."

"The blood is dry, but the finger looks, um, pretty fresh," Clay states. "There's an envelope inside the box, too," he adds.

"And that means what, Clay?" Ivey asks him, even though they all already know the answer.

"It means Henry Lawton didn't do this. Vidar is still out there."

"Don't jump to conclusions," Chief Wells tells Clay. "Maybe Lawton has an accomplice."

"And maybe I know who this finger belongs to," Hannah interrupts. "Ivey, help Clay remove that ring!"

While Clay and Ivey carefully follow Hannah's instructions, she starts updating the MIT about Landon Mead's connection to the lawsuit.

"And," she concludes, "Mrs Mead isn't taking my calls."

"Hannah!" Clay calls out. "There's an engraving inside. It says, 'For Landon, till death do us part, Sarah.'"

"Yolanda? Send a team to the Mead home on the double," Quinn orders. "And Clay, open that envelope!"

Clay does as Quinn says and finds a photograph and a message from Vidar inside. Clay's voice trembles as he reads it out loud.

"Dear Dr Sheridan, can you and Inspector McGowan find Mr Mead in time? I've given you lots of clues already, and this photo is the last one. If it helps you, I'll see you soon. If not, you lose – and so does Landon Mead. Yours, Vidar."

Everyone starts bombarding him with questions and comments, but Clay ignores them. He's staring at the old black and white photograph. It shows two young boys standing next to a horse in front of a huge manor house.

"Chief Wells, I need to speak with Harry Lawton. Now."

Exercise 53: Odd one out. Welches Wort ist das „schwarze Schaf"? Unterstreichen Sie!

1. snap   bark   purr   shout
2. suggestion   regulation   procedure   rule
3. manor   town   bed-sit   cottage
4. immediately   on the double   right away   later

Just 15 minutes later, Clay enters the interrogation room where Henry Lawton is sitting with the solicitor. Chief Wells isn't happy about it, but Clay has insisted on going in alone.

"Mr Lawton? I'm Dr Clay Sheridan. Do you recognize me?"

"No. Should I? And why are you here? I don't need a doctor. No nosebleeds today."

"I'm not a medical doctor, Mr Lawton. I'm a psychologist who works as a behavioural investigative advisor with the police."

"Well, I don't need a shrink, either. I just need to get out of here!"

"Perhaps I can help you with that. But first, you have to help me. I'd like you to tell me about this picture," Clay says and puts

manor house	Herrenhaus, Landsitz
⚡ shrink	Seelenklempner

the photo on the table so Lawton can see it.

"Oh! Where in the world did you find this?"

Lawton sounds surprised, but Clay thinks he hears something else in the man's voice. Nervousness? Or is it fear?

"Never mind that now. But the older boy on the left is you, isn't it?"

"Yes. I must have been, what, around 10 or 11."

"And where are you in the photo?"

Exercise 54: Passive voice. Lesen Sie weiter und setzen Sie die Verben ins Passiv!

"The photo **1.** take _____ at the old Darlington Manor here in Sheffield," Lawton explains. "Not long after, it **2.** burn _____ to the ground. My parents **3.** employ _____ by the Darlingtons. Mum **4.** hire _____ as a cook and Dad worked in their steel factory. Though that **5.** close down _____ ages ago. It was really sad."

"What was really sad?" Clay asks.

"Oh, the fire. Miss Valerie Darlington died in it. And of course after that, both my parents were out of work."

101

to be like two peas in a pod	sich gleichen wie ein Ei dem anderen
live-in	im selben Haus wohnend
odd	seltsam, merkwürdig
to make fun of	sich lustig machen über
limp	Hinken
to flip through	durchblättern
circumstances *pl*	Umstände
to suffocate	ersticken

"Oh, how terrible. But tell me about the younger boy? You two look a lot alike."

"Yeah, like two peas in a pod, my father used to say. But why is this important, anyway?"

Clay's pulse is beating faster. He ignores Lawton's question. "Will you tell me the boy's name, Mr Lawton?"

"Victor. Victor Jones. His mother, Iris, was the Darlington's live-in housekeeper."

"And were you and Victor good friends, Mr Lawton?"

"Friends? No. Victor was about six years younger than me. He was an odd kid, but at least he never made fun of my missing toe. He had a birth defect on one of his feet, too. Anyway, he and his mum moved away after the fire. I haven't seen him since. But..."

"But what?" Clay asks excitedly. He senses he's close to finding out the meaning of Vidar's clue.

"Well, I can't be sure, but like I told that lady copper, there was a man that hired me to deliver some packages. And now that I think of it, he reminded me a little bit of Victor. They both had those dark-blue, almost purple eyes – and my client also walked with a bit of a limp."

"Thank you, Mr Lawton. You've been a big help."

As Clay rushes out of the interrogation room, he's already taking out his phone and calling Quinn. The DCI is still in a meeting with the MIT. He takes the call from Clay just as the profiler goes

102

into the room where Hannah, Ivey and Chief Wells have been watching and listening to him talk to Lawton. Impatiently, Clay motions for them to be quiet.

Exercise 55: In other words. Lesen Sie weiter und ersetzen Sie die Ausdrücke mit den angegebenen Alternativen!

theory   correct   team   trace   pay attention

"Quinn, **1.** listen carefully _____.
I need Doreen and her **2.** crew _____ to
3. track down _____ an Iris Jones and her
son, Victor – the other boy in the photo. If my **4.** suspicion
_____ is **5.** right _____, Vidar has
sent us an old picture of himself!"

"What! Okay, Iris and Victor Jones. Got it. Anything else? Wait a minute. Doreen wants to talk to you. I'll put the loudspeaker on."
"Clay? The name Iris Jones came up in our HOLMES search for previous victims. Hold on a second."
Clay hears Doreen flipping through some papers.
"Okay, I've found it. Iris Jones died under mysterious circumstances 12 years ago. She's on the HOLMES cross-check because her body was missing the thumb on her right hand."
"What was the cause of death, Doreen?"
"She suffocated. There was a fire at her home in Leeds."
"Another fire," Hannah says thoughtfully.

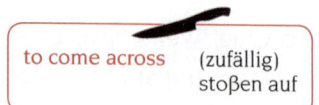

to come across | (zufällig) stoßen auf

"Was that Hannah?" Quinn asks. "What does she mean?"

"Well, Lawton just told Clay that a fire destroyed the place where the photo was taken – and where Iris Jones used to work. A place called Darlington Manor."

"Darlington?" Quinn exclaims. "I've come across that name recently. It's in the background report about Estelle Ashworth! Her father married a woman named Julie Darlington – and adopted his second wife's child, Valerie."

"But that means the woman who died in the fire was Estelle Ashworth's stepsister," Hannah gasps.

"I remember Valerie Darlington," the Chief adds. "But not from here. I grew up in London and my mum took me to one of Valerie Darlington's piano concerts there when I was a boy."

"Valerie Darlington was a pianist?" Clay asks, and in his mind's eye, he sees the image of Malcolm Ashworth's mutilated body at the grand piano in the Ashworth home.

His brain is working feverishly trying to put all the pieces together, when finally something clicks.

"Chief Wells, will you authorize and arrange a search of the Darlington property? That could be where Vidar is holding Landon Mead."

"Yes. I can be there with two armed response vehicles[i] and search dogs in half an hour."

"Then let's go," Hannah says excitedly.

"Oh no, Inspector McGowan. You and Dr Sheridan aren't going anywhere. Vidar has threatened you both – I'm not taking any chances."

Polizisten sind in Großbritannien normalerweise nicht bewaffnet. **Armed Response Vehicles** (ARV) sind besonders ausgestattete Polizeifahrzeuge bewaffneter Polizeieinheiten für den Einsatz in gefährlichen Situationen.

104

Exercise 56: Who's who? Finden Sie die gesuchten Charaktere und enträtseln Sie das Lösungswort!

1. Estelle's stepsister ☐ __ __ __ __ __ __

2. MIT leader __ __ ☐ __ __ __ __ __ __ __ __

3. Ed Jenkin's job ☐ __ __ __ __ __ __ __ __

4. the suspect's surname __ __ __ ☐ __ __

5. Ivey's surname __ __ __ __ ☐

6. a Norse god __ __ __ __ ☐

Lösung: ☐ ☐ ☐ ☐ ☐ ☐

8 BURIED SECRETS

Estelle is upstairs in her room at the Ashworth townhouse when the doorbell rings just before 11 a.m. She hasn't left her bedroom since she got home from hospital on Monday afternoon.

The housekeeper, Helen, keeps bringing ⓘ up tea and small things to eat, but Estelle can't face the thought of food. Instead she's trying to drown her sorrows in the new bottles of vodka she had delivered yesterday. But no matter how much she drinks, Estelle can't forget what has happened to Malcolm, Neal and that judge – and her own role in their horrid deaths. It's almost a relief when Helen knocks on the

to face sth.	*hier*: etw. ertragen
to drown one's sorrows	seine Sorgen ertränken
horrid	entsetzlich, grauenhaft
encore	Zugabe
cart	*hier*: Gerätewagen
to gather one's courage	seinen Mut zusammennehmen

Folgt nach **to keep** ein zweites Verb, so steht dieses wie hier immer in der **ing-Form**, z.B. *to keep smiling*. Nach „to keep" folgt also nie ein Infinitiv.

door and tells her that DCI Baxter is downstairs.

"Tell him I'll come down in a few minutes. And Helen, would you mind making us both some tea."

When Helen leaves, Estelle slowly gets out of bed and goes to look at herself in the mirror. She hates what she sees there.

106

Exercise 57: Adjectives. Lesen Sie weiter und unterstreichen Sie alle acht Adjektive!

"She was truly beautiful, wasn't she?" Vidar says in a low voice to Landon Mead.

The killer is pinning up a life-sized copy of a photo of Valerie Darlington onto the hard stone wall opposite the dirty mattress.

"This is one of my favourite photos of her," Vidar continues. "It was taken during her last concert. As an encore, she played a song especially for me. Do you want to hear it?"

Landon is so terrified and confused that he can't speak. He just nods his head and Vidar goes over to a cart he's rolled into the room. It's filled with hi-fi equipment and a flat screen. Brahms' Lullaby fills the small room and Vidar closes his eyes as he begins to hum the melody. Soon his face is wet with tears.

Landon is surprised by the tears in his own eyes. Oh Valerie, he sighs. He doesn't realize he's said her name out loud until Vidar begins screaming.

"Don't you dare say her name! You're one of the reasons she's dead!"

"Why... what do you mean?" Landon's voice is trembling. He tries to gather his courage. "And what do you have to do with Va... her anyway?"

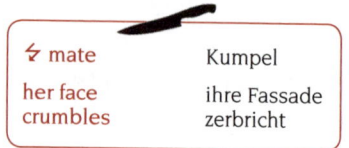

⚡ mate	Kumpel
her face crumbles	ihre Fassade zerbricht

"You'll find out soon, Mr Mead. But it's time for you to talk now. You're going to tell me what happened that night at Darlington Manor, just like your friend Neal Walsh did – before I killed him."

"What? Neal is dead?"

"Oh, of course. You haven't seen the news in a while. Yes, I killed him, together with your mate Malcolm Ashcroft and that old judge, John Kinkaid, too. I killed them with this," Vidar says with an evil smile and takes out the axe that he had hidden behind the monitor.

Exercise 58: Using new words. Vervollständigen Sie die Sätze mit Vokabeln aus dem Text!

1. He loaded all the heavy objects onto the ▮▮▮▮▮ so he could move them.

2. Musicians may give an ▮▮▮▮▮ at the end of a concert.

3. She held her baby son and sang a ▮▮▮▮▮ to him.

4. Mead showed a great deal of ▮▮▮▮▮ when he confronted Vidar.

5. I've know Johnny since we were kids. He's still my best ▮▮▮▮▮.

108

Quinn hears Estelle coming down the stairs, but he doesn't turn to look at her. He's standing at the grand piano next to where the MP's body was. Other than the fact that the body is gone, the crime scene looks almost the same as it did on Sunday morning.

"DCI Baxter? You wanted to see me?"

Quinn ignores Estelle while he takes something out of his pocket and places it on the piano. It's the heart-shaped picture frame – only it isn't empty anymore.

"It's a fine picture of your stepsister, Valerie Darlington. Isn't it, Mrs Ashworth?"

At first, Estelle just stares silently at the photo. Then her face crumbles.

"The one that used to be in the frame was better," she says in a tired voice. "It showed Valerie looking... gentle and kind."

Then Estelle's voice hardens. ⓘ "How did you find out?"

"It was Dr Sheridan's idea to copy a photo of your stepsister from an old newspaper and put it in the frame," Quinn explains. "To be honest, I don't know how he made the connection."

"So you don't know everything about Valerie – and what happened to her – to us?"

"No, Mrs Ashworth. But you have to tell me now. It might just help us save a life."

Das Verb **to harden** (hart werden) leitet sich vom Adjektiv **hard** ab. Es gibt im Englischen viele weitere Verben, die so gebildet werden, z.B. *tighten, loosen, broaden, soften, weaken* usw.

Landon is still trying to take in the fact that Malcolm, Neal and Judge Kinkaid are all dead. He's horrified, and the sight of the axe has made him too scared to ask Vidar for details. And as usual, his biggest concern is for himself.

109

Exercise 59: Unscramble the dialogue. Lesen Sie weiter und bringen Sie den Dialog zwischen Landon und Vidar in die richtige Reihenfolge!

a) "Why is that damned fire so important to you?" Landon asks.

b) "As were Malcolm and Estelle Ashworth, Neal Walsh – and my mother," he adds.

c) "Maybe. That depends on what you tell me about the fire."

d) "Because I was there! And so were you!" Vidar shouts.

e) "Are you... are you going to kill me, too?"

1	2	3	4	5

"But you must have been a small child then," Landon says in surprise. "Who... of course! You're Victor, the housekeeper's little boy! What was her name?

"Iris Jones," Vidar says flatly. "But *my* name is Vidar now, and I want you to stop asking questions and start giving me answers! Now tell me, which one of you bastards crushed Valerie's hand?"

"The coroner's report says almost all the bones in Valerie Darlington's right hand were broken," Hannah tells Clay. "The cause is unknown."

Clay and Hannah are sitting close to each other at the police headquarters. While they wait impatiently for news from Ivey and Chief Wells, they are examining the old reports about the investigation into the Darlington Manor fire.

"It happened exactly about this time of year, back in November of 1975," Clay says and flips another page.

"Where did they find her body?" Hannah asks. "And why was she the only one who didn't manage to get out of the house alive?"

"They found her in her room upstairs – the door was locked from the inside. As for the others, let me find the witness statements... Here they are."

"Bloody hell, Hannah! Look! Valerie Darlington was hosting a party that night to celebrate Malcolm Ashworth's twenty-first birthday. And the Meads and Neal Walsh were there, too! And Estelle, of course."

Hannah immediately starts texting Quinn with this new information. Perhaps he can use it during his interview with Mrs Ashworth, she thinks.

Suddenly, Clay puts down the report. He quickly pulls out his list of questions and notes about the three murders from his briefcase and starts adding more questions.

flatly	ausdruckslos
to crush	zerschmettern, zerquetschen
witness statement	Zeugenaussage
to host	veranstalten, Gastgeber sein

After he's done, he picks up his smartphone, goes online and calls up a map of Sheffield. He's looking at it with a frown on his face when Hannah finishes writing her message to Quinn.

She puts a hand on Clay's shoulder and looks down at what he's written.

111

Exercise 60: Translation. Übersetzen Sie Clays Fragen auf Deutsch!

1. Is Victor's / Vidar's own birth defect part of his motive?

   _____

   _____

2. Did he kill his own mother, Iris Jones? If so, why?

   _____

   _____

3. What is the connection to the toxic waste victims?

   _____

   _____

4. Where did Vidar's story really begin?

   _____

"I don't really know where to start, DCI Baxter," Estelle says quietly, "or if telling this old, tragic story can help Landon."

Quinn has told her about the notes and packages that Sarah Mead and Clay have received.

"Valerie was 12 and I was 14 when my father married her mother, Julie Darlington. My own mum had died when I was a baby, and Valerie's father, Jim Darlington, was also dead. After the marriage we moved to Darlington Manor and my father helped Julie

112

run her family's steel factory. My dad adopted Valerie and I was hoping that she would be the younger sister I'd always wanted. That we'd be a real family..."

Estelle pauses and looks at the photograph again. "But it didn't turn out that way. Valerie was a child prodigy and her mother had completely spoiled her. Valerie had already started winning piano competitions, and everything was about her – and her tantrums. She terrorized us."

"Were you jealous of her?"

"Not at first. I admired her and her talent. But when she turned 15, she discovered her other passion: sex."

child prodigy	Wunderkind
to spoil sb.	jmd. verwöhnen, jmd. verziehen
competition	Wettbewerb
tantrum	Wutanfall, Tobsuchtsanfall
promiscuous	sexuell freizügig
to be obsessed with	bessesen sein von
conquest	Eroberung

"Are you saying she was promiscuous?"

"No, more than that. She was obsessed with wrapping every male in sight around her little finger. Back then, her conquests included factory workers, her piano teacher and my boyfriend."

"Malcolm Ashworth."

"Yes. And his best friends, too. Neal Walsh and Landon Mead."

"I don't know what happened to her hand!" Landon cries out. "I was drunk that night – we all were, especially Valerie."

Landon stops talking for a moment to see if Vidar is going to start shouting again because he's said her name. But he doesn't.

"Yes, I know. I was sleeping in my room two floors above, but you were all so loud, it woke me up. I heard screaming."

Exercise 61: Simple or Progressive form? Lesen Sie weiter und übersetzen Sie die Verben richtig!

"Valerie [**1. spielen**] _____ the piano for us all - the same song you [**2. spielen**] _____ now," Landon continues. "Suddenly, she just [**3. scheinen**] _____ to go completely crazy. She [**4. anfangen**] _____ hammering the keys with her hands, and all the time she [**5. schreien**] _____ at Estelle that she was going to tell the truth. She screamed that she [**6. nicht leben können**] _____ a lie anymore."

"Iris – your mother – came running, and Malcolm helped the two of them drag Valerie out of the room and up the stairs. That was the end of the party. Sarah, Neal and I left then. I never saw Valerie alive again."

"But I did. She came into my room much later that night. Her hand was already bandaged. It must have hurt really badly. But she bent down and kissed me and said she was sorry, so sorry."

Landon is holding his breath. Vidar seems to be in some kind of trance now. Landon wonders if he can take advantage of it somehow. But no, the killer suddenly realizes he's losing control.

"I didn't understand what she meant until a few years ago when I discovered this in our house in Leeds," he says and takes out a small book from his pocket. "It's Valerie's diary."

At police headquarters, Hannah and Clay are discussing his new questions when Clay's phone rings. It's Chief Wells. Clay places the phone between his and Hannah's ears so she can listen in.

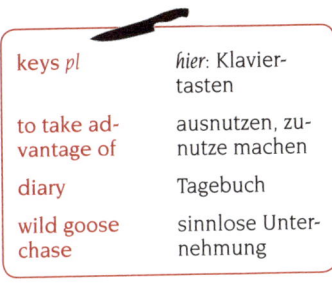

keys pl	hier: Klavier-tasten
to take advantage of	ausnutzen, zu-nutze machen
diary	Tagebuch
wild goose chase	sinnlose Unternehmung

"Dr Sheridan, you sent us on a wild goose chase. We've searched the entire Darlington property and there's no sign of Vidar or Landon Mead."

"I'm sorry, Chief. But listen, I have another idea..."

"Keep it to yourself! Maybe Scotland Yard has resources to waste, but the South Yorkshire budget doesn't have enough funds for anymore profiler nonsense!"

The Chief hangs up angrily and Hannah and Clay look at each other in disappointment.

"Hannah, do you trust me?"

"What a stupid question, Clay. Of course I do. Last night wouldn't have happened if I didn't"

"Good," he smiles and kisses her quickly.

Then he takes his car key out of his coat pocket. "I want to check something. It may seem a little crazy. I'll explain on the way."

"Where are we going?" Hannah asks as they hurry to the car.

"Back to the beginning – the place that I think will bring all the angles of Vidar's story together."

115

Exercise 62: Idiom matching. Wie lauten die Redewendungen richtig? Ordnen Sie zu!

1. ☐ to be like   **a)** a wild goose chase

2. ☐ to jump   **b)** your sorrows

3. ☐ to drown   **c)** red-handed

4. ☐ to go on   **d)** two peas in a pod

5. ☐ to be caught   **e)** before pleasure

6. ☐ to put business   **f)** to conclusions

"I'm afraid, though, I won't be able to read the diary to you in person, Mr Mead," Vidar tells Landon. "It's time for me to leave and start using the money from your – and the others' bank accounts. Now I won't have to work my fingers to the bone in computer programming anymore. And the other victims will also finally be getting the compensation they deserve."

Landon has no idea what Vidar means by "other victims" – and doesn't dare to ask. He watches the killer turn around and go over to the hi-fi equipment. Vidar switches on the monitor and hits the play button on a remote control. A video of Vidar sitting in an old-fashioned, wooden rocking chair appears on the screen. In one hand, he's holding Valerie's diary and in the other one, a heart-shaped frame. In the room, Vidar turns up the volume as loud as it will go just as his recorded self begins talking.

"This picture shows Valerie holding me," Vidar's voice booms out from the video. "She's 17 and I was just a few days old. She wrote

116

about that day – and many others. I'm going to read to you now."

The volume is so loud that Landon raises his hands and covers his ears. But Vidar sees him and starts screaming again. "No! You have to listen. I want everyone to know the truth!"

to work one's fingers to the bone	sich die Finger wund arbeiten
compensation	Entschädigung
rocking chair	Schaukelstuhl
to boom	*hier*: dröhnen
abortion	Abtreibung
snobbery	Snobismus
determined	entschlossen

"Valerie found out she was pregnant just weeks after our parents died in a car crash," Estelle tells Quinn in a shaky voice. "She wouldn't say who the father was – maybe she didn't even know herself. She refused to have an abortion or to have the baby adopted."

Suddenly Quinn understands where this is going. "So you came up with the plan to have your housekeeper pretend that the child, Victor, was hers!"

"Yes. Back then an unmarried, teenaged mother would have been a huge scandal in our social circles. Not to mention what it would have done to Valerie's career as a concert pianist. For a woman of Iris's class, it didn't matter as much."

Quinn manages to stop himself from saying something rude about Estelle's snobbery.

"And the night of the fire?" he asks instead.

"That night, Valerie was so drunk and determined to tell the truth. Iris, Malcolm and I managed to get her out of the room and upstairs. But when I slammed the door to her room, Valerie's hand was caught between the door and its frame and..."

Estelle's voice is trembling and she is trying not to cry.

"And what, Mrs Ashworth?" Quinn encourages her to go on.

mole	*hier*: Muttermal
to inherit	erben
estate	*hier*: Nachlass
deserted	verlassen
to cast shadows	Schatten werfen
gloomy	düster
shiny	glänzend, glitzernd
storage shed	Lagerschuppen
solar PV panel	Photovoltaik-anlage

"The sound of the bones breaking was the worst thing I've ever heard – except, of course, for Valerie's moans of agony. It wasn't the physical pain. She knew she'd never play the piano again."

"And was she the one who..."

"Yes. Valerie wouldn't let us help her and she locked herself in her room. That's where the fire started. I'll never know if it was an accident or not. But it was my fault, really. Mine – and Malcolm's."

"He was the father, then?"

"Yes. We never had a blood test done, of course. But Victor has a mole on his upper right thigh – exactly like the one Malcolm has... had."

"Is that why Iris Jones and Victor moved to Leeds after the fire?"

"Yes, partly. I gave Iris a lot of money and bought her a house. And since my father had adopted Valerie, I was her only living relative. Legally, Victor was Iris' child, so I inherited Valerie's estate – including this townhouse."

"But somehow, Victor learned the truth and is taking revenge."

"And he is taking back his inheritance."

"You mean the money from your husband's bank accounts?"

"And from mine, too. They're empty. I'll have to sell this place."

Um im Konjunktiv unwahrscheinliche Wünsche oder Vorschläge auszudrücken, verwendet man wie hier das Verb in der einfachen Vergangenheit. Bei *be* wird für alle Personen *were* verwendet.

118

"Well, at least he didn't kill you, too," Quinn points out.

"I don't know why he didn't!" Estelle cries out. "He must hate me more than any of his victims. But right now, I wish I were dead, [i] too. Maybe that's what Victor wanted – for me to live with what I've done."

Estelle stares at the grand piano and finally lets the tears come.

Clay takes Hannah's hand as the two of them begin walking around what's left of the old Darlington steel factory. The place is deserted and the empty main factory building casts strange and gloomy shadows on the ground.

Exercise 63: Translation. Lesen Sie weiter und über-setzen Sie die Vokabeln. Achten Sie bei den Verben auf die korrekte Zeitform!

Elektrizität   Gespenster   fest   bemerken   zittern

Dach

Hannah **1.** _____. She doesn't really believe in

2. _____, but even so, she would not like to be

here on her own. Clay is holding onto her hand

3. _____. Then she suddenly **4.** _____

something shiny up on the **5.** _____ of an old

storage shed.

"Clay, look! Isn't that a solar PV panel - for generating

6. _____?"

jaw	Kiefer
wire	Draht
springs *pl*	(Sprung-)Federn
to recover	sich erholen
to miss	*hier*: verfehlen
to cringe	zusammenzucken
musty	muffig
hatch	Klappe, Luke

"Yes, you're right! And I don't think they had those back in the 1970s, did they?" Clay says.

"No, they certainly didn't! I'd like to get a closer look. But if Vidar is inside that building, I don't have a weapon. Maybe we should call Chief Wells and tell him about this."

"I don't think he'll listen to us. Wait."

Clay rushes back to the car, and when he returns, he's carrying a torch – and a gun.

Hannah gasps when she sees it.

"Don't worry, Hannah. I've got a licence for it – and," he adds grimly, "I know how to use it."

"Listen to her!" Vidar screams as he rushes to pull Landon's hands away from his ears. But suddenly Landon lets them fall and swings up his left hand in a hard, powerful punch. It lands on Vidar's jaw and sends him falling backwards. His head hits the corner of the metal cart and starts bleeding.

Landon moves as quickly as his chains allow him to. As he starts hopping towards Vidar, he pulls out the sharp wire he's removed from the mattress springs and had hidden up his shirt sleeve. He aims the wire at the killer's throat. But in the last second before Landon reaches him, Vidar recovers and rolls to the side. The wire just misses Vidar, but the force of the attack makes Landon fall and he lands hard on his knees. Both men are breathing heavily, and in the background the video is still playing.

120

"This will be the last entry in my diary," Vidar is reading aloud on the video screen. "I'm writing it with my left hand, and when it's finished, I'm giving it to Iris. One day when Victor is old enough, she should tell him who his mother and father really were. I hope he understands – and believes [i] how much I love him."

> Achtung, verwechseln Sie nicht das Verb **to believe** (glauben) mit dem Substantiv **belief** (Glaube)!
> Das Wortende wird beim Verb stimmhaft ausgesprochen, beim Substantiv dagegen stimmlos:
> **to believe** [bɪ'liːv] **belief** [bɪ'liːf]
> **to relieve** [rɪ'liːv] **relief** [rɪ'liːf]

Clay and Hannah approach the shed and cringe when the old, rusty door squeaks as they open it. It's dark inside and smells damp and musty. Hannah and Clay go slowly inside, but the room is empty.

Clay turns on the torch and they see a small, wooden hatch in the floor. It's partly open and the two of them suddenly hear faint sounds coming from beneath it.

"Clay!" Hannah whispers and pulls at his arm. "We have to get back-up. Now!"

But Clay shakes his head, walks towards the hatch and slowly starts to push it aside.

"Clay! Don't!"

Hannah knows that what they are doing goes against every police procedure, but she can't leave Clay here alone. Quickly, she takes out her phone and texts Chief Wells:

```
Need back-up at the old steel
factory. ASAP.
```

Then she follows Clay down the metal stairs into the darkness.

121

Exercise 64: Crossword puzzle. Lösen Sie das Kreuzworträtsel!

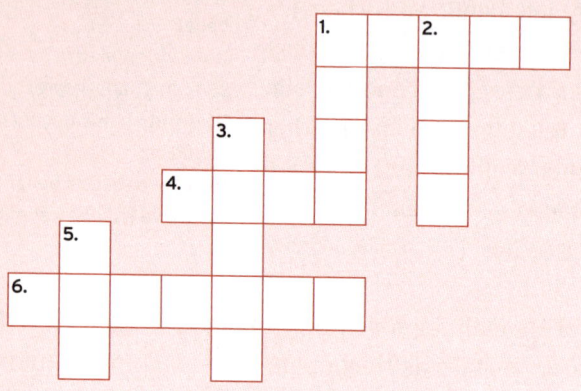

Across

1. smelling damp and unpleasant

4. Landon's weapon

6. childish way to show anger

Down

1. Malcolm and Vidar both have one on their bodies

2. small storage building

3. a book for writing secrets

5. a bone at the bottom of your face

Landon is terrified. What will Vidar do next now that Landon has tried to kill him? But the killer is staring at the monitor with a strange look of adoration on his face. Holding tightly to the wire,

Landon gathers his courage again and slowly sits down.

"And did you?" he dares to ask. "Did you understand?"

"Yes. It wasn't her fault that she couldn't **acknowledge** me as her child. It was the

adoration	Verehrung, Anbetung
acknowledge	anerkennen
to botch	verpfuschen
pathetically	kläglich, erbärmlich
to whirl around	herumwirbeln

others – Estelle, Malcolm... and Iris. Iris was outside chopping wood when I confronted her with the diary. She lied, and that made me even more furious. I grabbed the axe and made her tell me the truth." Vidar smiles triumphantly.

"She also told me why I'm missing two toes on my left foot. Valerie, my real mother, was here in Sheffield during her pregnancy. She often walked in the forest near the steel factory. It hadn't been closed that long and the pits full of toxic waste were still here."

Vidar's voice is getting higher and louder now.

"Those men who **botched** the clean-up and that judge deserved to die, too. Bone by bone, just like you will!" Victor screams hysterically.

He stands up and restarts the album on the turntable. Then he grabs his axe and raises it high above his head. Landon is also on his feet now and frantically hopping backwards towards the mattress, waving the piece of wire **pathetically** like a sword. Vidar laughs crazily as he slowly walks towards Landon. That's why he doesn't notice the door to the cell opening behind him. Landon does, though, and Vidar sees the look of relief in the terrified man's eyes.

"Put down the axe, Vidar!" Clay cries out. "It's over."

But Vidar **whirls around** and swings the axe down just as Clay fires the gun. Both weapons hit their targets. Vidar falls to the

123

floor, blood pouring out of his chest, as pain explodes in Clay's left arm.

"Clay!" Hannah screams as she comes running inside.

Landon Mead begins sobbing.

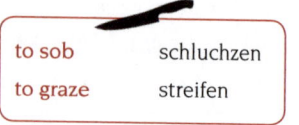

| to sob | schluchzen |
| to graze | streifen |

In a daze, Clay realizes that the axe has only grazed his arm.

And on the video, Vidar continues reading from his mother's diary as the music from Valerie's recording plays on.

Her son opens his eyes, looks at Clay and manages to murmur, "You win, Dr Sheridan. Lullaby... and goodnight... thy mother's..."

FINAL TEST

Exercise 1: Case facts. Welche Aussagen sind korrekt? Kreuzen Sie an!

1. Vidar was also a victim of the toxic waste. ❏

2. Victor always knew who his birth mother was. ❏

3. Hannah and Clay have been attracted to each other for ages. ❏

4. Quinn and Clay meet the first time at the Ashworth's. ❏

5. Estelle regrets what she did. ❏

6. Malcom Ashworth was Victor's father. ❏

Exercise 2: Odd one out. Welches Wort ist das „schwarze Schaf"? Unterstreichen Sie!

1. fault   blame   guilt   perp
2. limb   leg   knuckle   arm
3. grisly   tatty   horrid   gruesome
4. faint   blurry   fuzzy   distorted
5. clue   trace   cuff   evidence

Exercise 3: Opposites matching. Ordnen Sie die Adjektive ihrem Gegenteil zu!

1. ☐ reluctant
2. ☐ muffled
3. ☐ desirable
4. ☐ drained
5. ☐ hardly
6. ☐ faint

a) unattractive
b) enthusiastic
c) energetic
d) loud
e) strong
f) entirely

Exercise 4: Word forms. Wandeln Sie die Substantive um in Adjektive oder Adverbien und setzen Sie sie richtig ein!

liability   hazard   mystery   tenderness   mercy
controversy

1. "I think I know why he did it," he whispered _____.

2. Vidar was not _____ to any of his victims.

3. The judge ruled that the city was not _____.

4. Clay stroked Hannah _____ as she fell asleep in his arms.

5. Toxic waste is _____.

6. The MPs latest speeches were very _____.

126

Exercise 5: Mixed tenses. Bringen Sie die Verben in die richtige Vergangenheitsform!

The Met and Yorkshire police **1. collaborate** _____

in a VC when Vidar **2. reveal** _____ the shocking

murder of his third victim. Judge Kinkaid **3. kill** _____

the night before in Oxford, just hours after Vidar **4. chop**

_____ off the former Lord Mayor's hands and feet.

Neal Walsh's wife **5. visit** _____ their daughter at

the time, so she **6. not help** _____ him.

Exercise 6: Definitions. Vervollständigen Sie die Definitionen!

1. Someone who commits _____ kills themselves.
2. To drink slowly is to _____ . The opposite is to _____ .
3. Elderly people who no longer work have _____ .
4. The two words to describe the sex of men and women are _____ and _____ .
5. A _____ hangs from a ceiling and holds lights or candles.

Exercise 7: Questions about the text. Jetzt kennen Sie die ganze Geschichte. Beantworten Sie die Fragen zum Text!

1. Why does Estelle Ashworth think Vidar let her live?

2. Why do you think Victor chose to call himself "Vidar"?

3. Why doesn't Hannah like Ivey?

4. Name Vidar's motives for killing and mutilating his victims.

Exercise 8: Bone by Bone. Vervollständigen Sie anhand der Hinweise die Redewendungen mit **bone** und finden Sie das Lösungswort!

1. to be bone __ __ ☐ __ __   (exhausted)

2. __ __ __ __ __ ☐ __ to the bone   (very shocked)

3. to __ __ ☐ __ a bone to pick with sb. (angry with sb.)

4. to work one's __ __ __ __ ☐ __ __ to the bone   (work very hard)

5. to be __ __ __ ☐ and bone   (very thin)

6. to have a __ __ __ __ __ __ ☐ in one's bones   (to sense sth. instinctively)

7. to be cut to __ __ ☐ bone   (deeply hurt, upset)

Lösung: ☐ ☐ ☐ ☐ ☐ ☐ ☐

ANSWERS

Exercise 1: 1. c 2. d 3. a 4. b

Exercise 2: 1. long 2. yellow 3. black 4. wet 5. thick 6. expensive

Exercise 3: 1. walks 2. re-lights 3. turns 4. checks 5. ignores 6. climb

Exercise 4: 1. false (It takes a few moments until he recognizes the man's eyes.) 2. false (He tells Malcolm he has never been better.) 3. true 4. false (He takes his time rearranging the room and looking at his work.)

Exercise 5: 1. him 2. her 3. herself 4. she 5. her

Exercise 6: 1. a 2. b 3. a 4. a

Exercise 7: 1. here (hear) 2. to (too) 3. before (befour) 4. Who (Where) 5. quite (quiet) 6. isn't (is)

Exercise 8: 1. pity 2. nightmare 3. coroner 4. fault 5. nightcap 6. gloves 7. blade 8. adversary **Lösung:** profiler

Exercise 9: 1. adds 2. means 3. set up 4. want 5. to question 6. tries

Exercise 10: 1. road block 2. enquiries 3. crime scene 4. orders

Exercise 11: 1. Estimated 2. wounds 3. weapon 4. mutilated 5. stumps 6. Perp(s)

130

Exercise 12: 1. motorway 2. centre 3. autumn 4. car park 5. motor 6. trouser 7. boot

Exercise 13: 1. sick 2. disoriented 3. happening 4. wearing 5. widen

Exercise 14: 1. No, he's a former Lord Mayor.
2. Yes, the killer says so.
3. No, not yet.
4. No, first he wants Neal to tell him about something that happened one night in the past.

Exercise 15: 1. are doing 2. are looking 3. are checking 4. needs 5. is preparing 6. helps

Exercise 16:

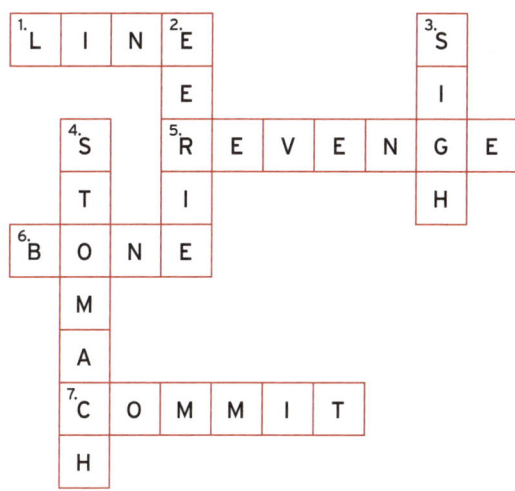

Exercise 17: 1. wives 2. technologies 3. fists 4. men

Exercise 18: 1. isn't it 2. can I 3. don't you 4. shouldn't you 5. won't you

Exercise 19: 1. c 2. d 3. a 4. b

131

Exercise 20: **1.** back **2.** on **3.** at **4.** for **5.** after **6.** without **7.** for

Exercise 21: **1.** No, she clearly recognizes the picture frame but says she doesn't.
2. Yes, Clay thinks Hannah is pretty and intelligent, and Hannah wants to spend time with Clay.
3. Yes, Estelle says Sarah should 'keep an eye on her own husband'.
4. Yes, he wants to spend time with his wife Betty.

Exercise 22: **1.** sleepily **2.** quick **3.** well **4.** tired **5.** late

Exercise 23:

G	R	O	W	L	E	O	F	I
H	A	W	H	I	S	P	E	R
L	T	T	I	S	H	B	K	S
O	T	I	M	M	O	A	N	C
X	L	Z	P	R	U	Q	J	R
D	E	T	E	O	T	U	L	E
A	Y	A	R	B	A	R	K	A
G	A	S	P	U	N	T	E	M
E	M	P	W	S	I	G	H	N

Exercise 24: **1.** MIT **2.** incident **3.** ASAP **4.** Victim **5.** politician **6.** butchered **7.** message

Exercise 25: **1.** already **2.** never **3.** just **4.** yet **5.** for

Exercise 26: **1.** d – To start with **2.** e – For example
3. c – Furthermore **4.** a – On the one hand
5. f – But on the other hand **6.** b – Now let's move on to

Exercise 27: 1. appear 2. hobby 3. victim 4. recorder

Exercise 28: 1. lucky 2. at 3. There is 4. man's 5. is trying 6. too

Exercise 29: 1. rang, rung 2. fell, fallen 3. took, taken 4. held, held 5. felt, felt 6. hit, hit

Exercise 30: 1. face falls 2. dancing to their tune 3. split second 4. a bite to eat

Exercise 31: 1. is coming 2. say 3. asking 4. have heard

Exercise 32:

1 O	2 V	3 E	4 R	5 E	6 S
20 R	21 E	22 L	23 U	24 C	7 I
19 O	32 I	33 T	34 O	25 T	8 D
18 T	31 R	36 Y	35 R	26 A	9 E
17 I	30 R	29 E	28 T	27 N	10 N
16 C	15 I	14 L	13 O	12 S	11 T

Exercise 33: 1. bone tired 2. angrily 3. to bother 4. to brief 5. grim 6. TV/television 7. to imagine 8. delight

Exercise 34: 1. obsessed with 2. interrogate 3. order 4. rush 5. investigate

Exercise 35: 1. The suspect was asleep when the police arrived.
2. Henry is not carrying a weapon.
3. The attractive copper has a search warrant.
4. Inspector Munro is looking for incriminating evidence.

133

Exercise 36: 1. didn't create 2. did 3. reminds 4. hired 5. clean up

Exercise 37: 1. c 2. d 3. a 4. b

Exercise 38: 1. families 2. area 3. packages/parcels 4. homes 5. courier 6. boss

Exercise 39: 1. The employer reported that Lawton had been on sick leave.
2. The suspect said he had a job on the side.
3. Lawton admitted that he knew some of the families.
4. Lawton claimed that he had been contacted through his homepage.

Exercise 40: 1. negligent 2. fault 3. lawyer 4. toxic waste 5. ruling 6. brownfield 7. twins
Lösung: lawsuit

Exercise 41: 1. through 2. at 3. with 4. to 5. up 6. out

Exercise 42: 1. c 2. e 3. b 4. d 5. a

Exercise 43: 1. want 2. accommodation 3. made 4. view 5. their 6. each other 7. caught

Exercise 44: 1. really 2. delicious 3. fine 4. politely 5. tight

Exercise 45: 1. How 2. Why 3. What 4. Is/Was 5. Whose

Exercise 46: 1. said (told) 2. used (use) 3. themselves (themself) 4. has stopped (stops) 5. thinks (means) 6. problems (problem)

Exercise 47:

A	S	D	S	M	E	C	I	D	M
W	A	I	T	E	R	H	S	I	A
S	A	L	A	D	F	E	R	M	C
O	T	V	R	N	C	E	N	E	X
R	E	S	T	A	U	R	A	N	T
D	Q	U	E	X	T	S	L	U	P
E	M	R	R	G	L	H	E	E	U
R	D	K	O	J	E	N	O	B	B
I	S	E	W	D	R	I	N	K	S
W	H	I	S	K	Y	A	U	G	O

Exercise 48: 1. notices 2. finally 3. getting to know 4. at least 5. agrees 6. share

Exercise 49: 1. hair is, a little 2. pale, wire-framed glasses 3. tall, weighs

Exercise 50: 1. looks at 2. arrived 3. has read 4. can't believe 5. picks up

Exercise 51: 1. instruction, to instruct 2. access, to access 3. finances, to finance 4. investigation, to investigate

Exercise 52: 1. in 2. at 3. up 4. with 5. on

Exercise 53: 1. purr 2. suggestion 3. town 4. later

Exercise 54: 1. was taken 2. was burnt 3. were employed 4. had been hired 5. was closed down

Exercise 55: 1. pay attention 2. team 3. trace 4. theory 5. correct

Exercise 56: 1. Valerie 2. Quinn Baxter 3. constable
4. Lawton 5. Munro 6. Vidar
Lösung: Victor

Exercise 57: 1. beautiful 2. low 3. life-sized 4. hard
5. opposite 6. dirty 7. favourite 8. last

Exercise 58: 1. cart 2. encore 3. lullaby 4. courage 5. mate

Exercise 59: 1. e 2. c 3. a 4. d 5. b

Exercise 60: 1. Ist Victors/Vidars eigener Geburtsfehler
Teil seines Motivs?
2. Hat er seine eigene Mutter, Iris Jones,
umgebracht? Falls ja, warum?
3. Was ist die Verbindung zu den Giftmüll-
opfern?
4. Wo fing Vidars Geschichte tatsächlich an?

Exercise 61: 1. was playing 2. are playing 3. seemed
4. started 5. was shouting 6. couldn't live

Exercise 62: 1. d 2. f 3. b 4. a 5. c 6. e

Exercise 63: 1. shivers/is shivering 2. ghosts 3. tightly
4. notices 5. roof 6. electricity

Exercise 64:

			1. M	U	2. S	T	Y
			O		H		
		3. D	L		E		
	4. W	I	R	E	D		
5. J		A					
6. T	A	N	T	R	U	M	
W		Y					

FINAL TEST

Exercise 1: 1. true 2. false (He learned this when he found Valerie's diary.) 3. false (Clay wonders why he never noticed it before.) 4. false (They go back a long way.) 5. true 6. true

Exercise 2: 1. perp 2. knuckle 3. tatty 4. faint 5. cuff

Exercise 3: 1. b 2. d 3. a 4. c 5. f 6. e

Exercise 4: 1. mysteriously 2. merciful 3. liable 4. tenderly 5. hazardous 6. controversial

Exercise 5: 1. were collaborating 2. revealed 3. had been killed 4. had chopped 5. was visiting 6. could not

Exercise 6: 1. suicide 2. sip, gulp 3. retired 4. male, female 5. chandelier

Exercise 7: 1. Estelle thinks Vidar wants to force her to live with what she has done (and suffer).
2. Because Vidar is the name of the Norse god of revenge. And revenge is his motive.
3. She is jealous of Ivey because Ivey flirts with Clay and wears sexy clothes. At first she thinks Clay is interested in Ivey.
4. He wants to avenge the death of his real mother, Valerie Darlington and that Estelle, Malcolm and Iris had lied to him. He also wants to take revenge for the toxic waste scandal.

Exercise 8: 1. tired 2. chilled 3. have 4. fingers 5. skin 6. feeling 7. the
Lösung: revenge

GLOSSARY

⚡	= umgangssprachlich
pl	= Plural

abortion	Abtreibung
accomplice	Komplize/Komplizin
acknowledge	anerkennen
administrator	Verwaltungsangestellte(r)
adoration	Verehrung, Anbetung
adversary	Gegner
agenda	*hier*: Plan
agony	(Höllen-)Qual
ale	obergäriges Bier
angle	*hier*: Ermittlungsansatz, Blickwinkel
approvingly	anerkennend
ASAP (as soon as possible)	so schnell wie möglich
Ask away.	Fragen Sie nur!
to assume	ausgehen von
available	verfügbar
back and forth	vor und zurück
bare	nackt, barfuß, bloß
barking	Bellen

to beam	strahlen
to bear (bore, borne) sth.	etw. ertragen
to be caught red-handed	auf frischer Tat ertappt werden
bed-sit	möbliertes Zimmer
to be like two peas in a pod	sich gleichen wie ein Ei dem anderen
to be obsessed with	besessen sein von
to bet (bet, bet)	wetten
to be tempted to do sth.	versucht sein, etw. zu tun
BIA (Behavioural Investigative Advisor)	psychologische(r) Fall-analytiker(in)
birth defect	Geburtsfehler
blade	Klinge
to blame sb.	jmd. die Schuld geben
to blink	blinzeln
blood stain	Blutfleck
⚡ bloody	verflucht, verdammt
⚡ Bloody hell!	Ach du Scheiße!
blurry	unscharf, verschwommen
to boom	*hier*: dröhnen
bone tired	hundemüde
to botch	verpfuschen
to bother sb.	jmd. Sorgen bereiten, jmd. plagen
to brief sb.	jmd. kurz informieren
briefcase	Aktentasche
⚡ bugger	*hier*: Arschloch
business on the side	Nebengeschäft
to butcher	(ab)schlachten
cable ties *pl*	Kabelbinder
to call it a night	Feierabend machen

cane	Gehstock
careless	nachlässig, achtlos
cart	*hier*: Gerätewagen
case	Fall
to cast (cast, cast) shadows	Schatten werfen
to catch up with sb.	jmd. einholen
CCTV camera	Überwachungskamera
certain degree	gewisser Grad, gewisses Maß
chandelier	Kronleuchter
Chief of Police	Polizeichef(in)
child prodigy	Wunderkind
chilled to the bone	*hier*: völlig durchgefroren
chilling	erschreckend, ernüchternd
to chill sb. to the bone	jmd. bis ins Mark erschüttern
to chime	schlagen, läuten
to choke out	erstickt sagen
chopping block	Hackklotz
circumstances *pl*	Umstände
City Council	Gemeinderat
claim	Klage
to clench (one's fist)	die Faust ballen
clue	Hinweis, Indiz
to collaborate	zusammenarbeiten
to come across	(zufällig) stoßen auf
to comfort sb.	jmd. trösten
to commit a crime	ein Verbrechen begehen
to commit suicide	Selbstmord begehen
company	*hier*: Gesellschaft
compensation	Entschädigung
competition	Wettbewerb

complaint	Klage, Beschwerde
complainant	Kläger(in)
condolences *pl*	Beileid
to confirm	bestätigen
conquest	Eroberung
constable	Streifenpolizist(in)
controversial	umstritten
convinced	überzeugt
⚡ copper	Bulle
coroner	Rechtsmediziner
cottage	kleines Landhaus
council housing estate	Sozialwohnungsanlage
courier	Kurier
court	Gericht
coward	Feigling
crank call	Juxanruf
crime scene	Tatort
to cringe	zusammenzucken
cross index	Querverweis
crowd	Menschenmenge
to crush	zerschmettern, zerquetschen
cuff	Handschelle
to curse	*hier*: fluchen
curtly	barsch
to cut sb. to the bone	jmd. tief treffen
cutlery	Besteck
Dachshund	Dackel
damp	feucht
delighted	entzückt, erfreut
to dance to sb.'s tune	nach jds. Pfeife tanzen
deserted	verlassen

to deserve what's coming to one	kriegen, was man verdient
desirable	begehrenswert
determined	entschlossen
to devastate	zerstören, umhauen
device	Gerät
diary	Tagebuch
ϟ to dig (dug, dug) in	reinhauen, es sich schmecken lassen
disoriented	desorientiert, verwirrt
distorted	verzerrt
to divorce sb.	sich von jmd. scheiden lassen
ϟ to do (did, done) sb. in	jmd. abmurksen
to drag	ziehen, schleppen
drained	erschöpft, erledigt
to drop by	vorbeischauen
to drown one's sorrows	seine Sorgen ertränken
to drug sb.	jmd. betäuben, jmd. narkotisieren
eerie	unheimlich
elderly	älter, ältlich
encore	Zugabe
encouraging	ermutigend, aufmunternd
engraving	Gravierung
entertaining	*hier*: Gäste bewirten
entire	ganz
estate	*hier*: Nachlass
evidence	Beweise
evilly	böse
to exclaim	(überrascht) ausrufen
exhausted	erschöpft

142

expected	erwartet
to face sth.	*hier*: etw. ertragen
faint	blass, schwach
to faint	ohnmächtig werden
faithful	treu
fake	falsch, unecht
fault	Schuld, Fehler
firearms unit	bewaffnete Polizeieinheit
fist	Faust
flatly	ausdruckslos
⚡ fling	Techtelmechtel, kurze Affäre
to flip through	durchblättern
foolish	albern, dumm
for old times' sake	um der alten Zeiten willen
force	*hier*: Gewalt, Zwang
forensics	Spurensicherung, Kriminaltechnik
former	ehemalig
frantically	verzweifelt
freckled	sommersprossig
⚡ from high up	von ganz oben
to frown	die Stirn runzeln
furious	wütend, zornig
fuzzy	unklar, verschwommen
gag	Knebel
to gasp	nach Luft schnappen
to gather one's courage	seinen Mut zusammennehmen
gaze	Blick
Get a hold of yourself!	Reiß dich zusammen!
to give one's best to sb.	jmd. (liebe) Grüße ausrichten

gloomy	düster
to go back a long way	sich schon lange kennen
gossip	*hier*: Klatschtante
to grab	packen, greifen
grand piano	Flügel
to graze	streifen
to greet	begrüßen
grim	grimmig, düster
grisly	grausig, grässlich
to growl	knurren
gruesome	grausig, grauenhaft
guilt	Schuld
gulp	großer Schluck
handle	Griff
hardly	kaum
to harm	schaden, verletzen
hatch	Klappe, Luke
to have a bone to pick with sb.	mit jmd. ein Hühnchen zu rupfen haben
to have a clean record	nicht vorbestraft sein
to have a lie-in	ausschlafen
hazardous	gefährlich
headquarters	Zentrale, Hauptquartier
her face crumbles	ihre Fassade zerbricht
her face falls	sie ist sichtlich enttäuscht
to hiss	zischen
hit man	Auftragskiller
honesty	Ehrlichkeit
horrid	entsetzlich, grauenhaft
to host	veranstalten, Gastgeber sein
hot lead	heiße Spur

house-to-house enquiries *pl*	Anwohnerbefragung
to hum	summen
to ID sb.	jmd. identifizieren
to imagine	sich vorstellen
to imply	andeuten
impressive	imposant, beeindruckend
to improve	(sich) verbessern
in a daze	benebelt, benommen
inadequate	unzureichend, unangemessen
in advance	im Voraus
in a low voice	mit leiser Stimme
inappropriate	unangemessen
incident room	Einsatzzentrale
incriminating	belastend, verfänglich
to inherit	erben
insightful	aufschlussreich
to insist on	bestehen auf
intention	Absicht, Vorhaben
interrogation	Verhör, Befragung
to intervene	eingreifen
in unison	gleichzeitig
investigator	Ermittler(in)
item	Gegenstand
It's a pity...	Schade, dass...
It's worth it.	Es lohnt sich.
jaw	Kiefer
journey	Reise
to jump to conclusions	voreilige Schlüsse ziehen
to keep up appearances	den Anschein wahren
keys *pl*	*hier*: Klaviertasten

knock-out drops *pl*	K.o.-Tropfen
knuckle	Fingerknöchel
laundry room	Waschküche
lawsuit	Klage, Rechtstreit
leaky	undicht, leck
liable	verantwortlich, haftbar
limbs *pl*	Gliedmaßen
limp	Hinken
live-in	im selben Haus wohnend
long shot	weithergeholte Vermutung
Lord Mayor	Oberbürgermeister(in)
low-cut	(tief) dekolletiert
lullaby	Wiegenlied
madman	Irrer, Verrückter
to make fun of	sich lustig machen über
male	*hier*: Mann
manor house	Herrenhaus, Landsitz
⚡ mate	Kumpel
merciful	gnädig
mess	Durcheinander, Sauerei
to miss	*hier*: verfehlen
to moan	stöhnen
mole	*hier*: Muttermal
mood	Laune, Stimmung
to move on	*hier*: weitermachen
MP (Member of Parliament)	Parlamentsabgeordneter (GB)
muffled	gedämpft
mug	Becher, Tasse
to murmur	murmeln
musty	muffig

146

mutilated	verstümmelt
nasty	fies, eklig
negligent	fahrlässig
nightcap	*hier*: Absacker, Schlummertrunk
nightmare	Albtraum
night shift	Nachtschicht
Norse	altnordisch
to not take any chances	kein Risiko eingehen
numerous	zahlreich
occasionally	gelegentlich
odd	seltsam, merkwürdig
old-fashioned	altmodisch
one-way glass	Spiegelglas
on sick leave	krankgeschrieben
on the double	sofort, im Eiltempo
ordinary	normal, gewöhnlich
to outdo (outdid, outdid) oneself	sich selbst übertreffen
outgoing	aufgeschlossen
pale	blass
paralyzed	(wie) gelähmt
passionate	leidenschaftlich
pathetically	kläglich, erbärmlich
pattern	Muster
paw	Pfote
peephole	Guckloch
⚡ perp (perpetrator)	Täter
to pick up	*hier*: empfangen
picture frame	Bilderrahmen
pinkie	kleiner Finger
⚡ pissed off	stinksauer, angepisst

pit	Grube
pity	Mitleid
plump	mollig, rundlich
pointedly	*hier*: demonstrativ
police contact management centre	Telefonbereitschaft der Polizei
promiscuous	sexuell freizügig
pulpy	breiig
punch	Schlag
to purr	schnurren
to put business before pleasure	erst die Arbeit und dann das Vergnügen
ragged breath	stoßweißer, unregelmäßiger Atem
to rattle	rasseln
recipient	Empfänger(in)
to recover	sich erholen
record	*hier*: Unterlagen
to regret	bedauern
regret	Bedauern
regulations *pl*	Vorschriften, Bestimmungen
reluctantly	ungern, widerwillig
to remind sb. of sth.	jdn. an etw. erinnern
remote control	Fernbedienung
resident	Bewohner(in), Anwohner(in)
respectable	anständig, respektiert
responsible	verantwortlich
retired	pensioniert
revenge	Rache
to review	überprüfen
revolving	sich drehend

to reward sb.	jmd. belohnen
to right sth.	etw. aufrichten
road block	Straßensperre
to rock	schaukeln
rocking chair	Schaukelstuhl
to rule against sb.	gegen jmd. entscheiden
ruling	Urteil
to rush	eilen, hetzen
saw dust	Sägemehl
scent	Duft, Geruch
scratched	zerkratzt
to scribble	kritzeln
search warrant	Durchsuchungsbefehl
security procedures *pl*	Sicherheitsschranken
to settle down	sich beruhigen
shapely	wohlgeformt
sharply	spitz, scharf
shiny	glänzend, glitzernd
to shiver	zittern, schlottern
⚡ shrink	Seelenklempner
to shrug	mit den Achseln zucken
to sigh in relief	erleichtert seufzen
to single sb. out	jmd. auswählen
sip	Schlückchen
slurred	undeutlich
to smash	niederschmettern
snobbery	Snobismus
to sob	schluchzen
softly	*hier*: leise
solar PV panel	Photovoltaikanlage
to soothe	beruhigen

to spare sb. sth.	jmd. etw. ersparen
special delivery	Eilzustellung, Sonderlieferung
to spill (spilt, spilt)	verschütten
spirit	*hier*: Mut, Kampfgeist
splendid	großartig, ausgezeichnet
split second	Sekundenbruchteil
to spoil sb.	jmd. verwöhnen, jmd. verziehen
springs *pl*	(Sprung-)Federn
to spurt	spritzen, schießen
stage	Bühne
to stand (stood, stood) out	auffallen, hervorstechen
starving	am Verhungern
to step out of line	aus der Reihe tanzen
storage shed	Lagerschuppen
to strangle	erwürgen
to struggle	kämpfen
study	Arbeitszimmer
stump	Stumpf, Stummel
stunned	fassungslos
to suffer	leiden
to suffocate	ersticken
supervisor	Vorgesetzte(r)
surveillance	Überwachung
survival instinct	Selbsterhaltungstrieb
to suspect	vermuten
to take advantage of	ausnutzen, zunutze machen
to take sth. in	etw. in Augenschein nehmen, erfassen
tantrum	Wutanfall, Tobsuchtsanfall
to target	*hier*: ins Visier nehmen

tatty	abgegriffen, zerfleddert
temptation	Versuchung
tender	zärtlich
territory	Gebiet
the old days	früher, in alten Zeiten
the pot calling the kettle black	ein Esel schimpft den anderen Langohr
This is it.	Das war's dann.
This round's on me!	Diese Runde geht auf mich!
threat	Drohung
tight schedule	knapper/straffer Zeitplan
⚡ tongue-lashing	Standpauke
toxic waste	Giftmüll
to trace sth.	etw. (zurück)verfolgen
to transfer	überweisen
to tremble	beben, zittern
tripod	Stativ
to trouble sb.	jmd. beunruhigen, jmd. Sorgen machen
to turn one's stomach	jmd. den Magen umdrehen
to turn sth. over to sb.	etw. übergeben an jmd. anderen
turntable	Plattenspieler
to twist away	sich wegdrehen
to twitch	zucken
Two can play at that game.	Wie du mir, so ich dir.
unconscious	bewusstlos
undue	*hier*: ungewollt
unsteady	unsicher, wackelig
victim	Opfer

to waste	verschwenden
webbed	mit Schwimmhäuten, verwachsen
⚡ What the devil!	Was zum Teufel!
to whimper	wimmern
to whirl around	herumwirbeln
to whisper	flüstern
wild goose chase	sinnlose Unternehmung
wire	Draht
witness statement	Zeugenaussage
to wonder	*hier*: sich fragen
to work one's fingers to the bone	sich die Finger wund arbeiten
wrist	Handgelenk
to yawn	gähnen
Yorkshire Pudding	traditionelle Beilage aus Teig zum Roast Beef

LIST OF EXERCISES

Mit Sprachen glänzen –
SilverLine für Schule, Studium und Beruf

13 Sprachen | 24 Reihen | 191 Titel

SilverLine Lernbox • SilverLine Sprachkurs einfach & aktiv • SilverLine Wörterbücher
SilverLine Kochen auf … • SilverLine Typische Fehler • SilverLine … leicht gemacht
SilverLine Business English Trainer • SilverLine Bildwörterbuch • SilverLine Kurzgrammatik
SilverLine Express • SilverLine 111 Sprachrätsel • SilverLine Business Update
SilverLine Die 2000 wichtigsten Wörter • SilverLine Sofort sprechen
SilverLine Sprachführer für die Reise • SilverLine Update

Compact Verlag GmbH
Baierbrunner Str. 27 · 81379 München · Tel. 089/74 51 61-0 · Fax 089/75 60 95
www.compactverlag.de · www.lernkrimi.de

Compact Lernkrimi
Classic

A1

A2

B1

Art and Ashes
ISBN 978-3-8174-8970-1

Cook and Kill
ISBN 978-3-8174-9492-7

Crime Scene Tower of London
ISBN 978-3-8174-7687-9

Deadly Mistake
ISBN 978-3-8174-8259-7

Death Wasn't the Deal
ISBN 978-3-8174-8968-8

Der Rächer von Canterbury
ISBN 978-3-8174-7662-6

Der rote Nebel
ISBN 978-3-8174-7574-2

Ein fast perfekter Coup
ISBN 978-3-8174-7568-1

Game Over in Soho
ISBN 978-3-8174-7878-1

Hunting the Vampire
ISBN 978-3-8174-7305-2

Komplott unter Palmen
ISBN 978-3-8174-7571-1

Schüsse im Nebel
ISBN 978-3-8174-7763-0

The Mystery of the Mummy
ISBN 978-3-8174-7304-5

Tod eines Dandys
ISBN 978-3-8174-7660-2

Toxic Testament
ISBN 978-3-8174-7879-8

Sammelband 3 in 1 (B1/B2)

Inspector Hudson Investigates
ISBN 978-3-8174-7625-1

London Crime Time
ISBN 978-3-8174-7787-6

B2

Bloody Diamonds
ISBN 978-3-8174-9494-1

Das geheimnisvolle Gemälde
ISBN 978-3-8174-7306-9

Der Seelenjäger
ISBN 978-3-8174-7581-0

Der unheimliche Ritter
ISBN 978-3-8174-7661-9

Die Rache des Lords
ISBN 978-3-8174-7663-3

Die Spur des Höllenhundes
ISBN 978-3-8174-7307-6

Lady Mayfair's Revenge
ISBN 978-3-8174-7815-6

Nobody Dies Twice
ISBN 978-3-8174-9495-8

Schatten der Vergangenheit
ISBN 978-3-8174-7570-4

The Riddle of the Black Shoe
ISBN 978-3-8174-7638-1

Business English

Das letzte Roulette
ISBN 978-3-8174-7609-1

Der 25-Millionen-Coup
ISBN 978-3-8174-7659-6

Teuflische Intrigen
ISBN 978-3-8174-7608-4

C1/C2

A Scottish Murder Mystery
ISBN 978-3-8174-8379-2

Compact Lernkrimi
Kurzkrimis

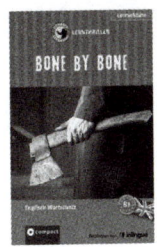

Compact Lernkrimi
Lernthriller

Compact Lernkrimi Kurzkrimis	Compact Lernkrimi Lernthriller	
The Murderer Next Door ISBN 978-3-8174-9438-5		**A1**
Blood and Breakfast ISBN 978-3-8174-7760-9 **Deadly Business** ISBN 978-3-8174-9215-2 **It Was Murder, My Lord** ISBN 978-3-8174-7734-0 **Last Exit Waterloo Bridge** ISBN 978-3-8174-7733-3 **Murder at Teatime** ISBN 978-3-8174-7839-2 <u>**Sammelband 10 in 1 (A2/B1)**</u> **Murderous Collection** ISBN 978-3-8174-8967-1		**A2**
Bullets over Bristol ISBN 978-3-8174-8544-4 **Death Comes Knocking** ISBN 978-3-8174-7945-0 <u>**American Business English**</u> **Murderous Network** ISBN 978-3-8174-9312-8	**Bone by Bone** ISBN 978-3-8174-9497-2 **Massacre United** ISBN 978-3-8174-9319-7 <u>**American English**</u> **Faceless Killer** ISBN 978-3-8174-8856-8	**B1**
	In Terror ISBN 978-3-8174-8857-5	**B2**
		C1/C2

Compact Lernkrimi
Rätselblock

Compact Lernkrimi
Hörbuch

	Compact Lernkrimi Rätselblock	Compact Lernkrimi Hörbuch
A1	**Murderous Games** ISBN 978-3-8174-9500-9	
A2	**The Art of Crime** ISBN 978-3-8174-9155-1	**A Shot in the Night** ISBN 978-3-8174-8202-3 **Death Wish** ISBN 978-3-8174-8204-7 **The Butterworth Mystery** ISBN 978-3-8174-8203-0
B1	**A Deadly Puzzle** ISBN 978-3-8174-8832-2	**Bloody Revenge** ISBN 978-3-8174-8860-5 **Danger at King's Cross** ISBN 978-3-8174-7673-2 **The Thames Murderer** ISBN 978-3-8174-7674-9
B2		**Bloody Legacy** ISBN 978-3-8174-7676-3 **Die Intrigantin** ISBN 978-3-8174-7675-6 <u>**Business English**</u> **Crime & Company** ISBN 978-3-8174-8976-3 **Murder at the Office** ISBN 978-3-8174-7747-0
C1/C2		

Compact Lernkrimi
Audio-Learning

Compact Lernkrimi
Sprachkurs

	Englisch für Anfänger (A1/A2) ISBN 978-3-8174-7784-5	A1
		A2
Totenstille im Hyde Park ISBN 978-3-8174-7797-5		B1
		B2
		C1/C2

Compact Lernkrimi
Spannend Sprachen lernen

Compact Lernkrimi Classic

› Spannende Krimistory mit über 70 Übungen

› Vokabel- und Infokästen direkt auf der Seite

ab 7,99 € (D)

Compact Lernkrimi Kurzkrimis

› Drei bzw. vier Kurzkrimis pro Band

› Ideal für den Einsatz an Schulen und VHS-Kursen

7,99 € (D)

Compact Lernkrimi Lernthriller

› Hochspannende Thriller mit Gänsehaut-Garantie

› 70 Übungen in ansteigendem Schwierigkeitsgrad

› Vokabel- und Infokästen

7,99 € (D)

Compact Lernkrimi Sammelband

› Drei Lernkrimis in einem Band mit über 300 Übungen

› Für mittleres bis fortgeschrittenes Sprachniveau

12,99 € (D)

Compact Lernkrimi Hörbuch

› Krimistory auf CD mit MP3-fähigen Tracks

› Begleitbuch zum Mitlesen inklusive Übungen und Vokabelangaben

9,99 € (D)

Compact Lernkrimi Audio-Learning

› Spannende Story im Buch

› Übungen zu Hörverständnis und Aussprache auf CD

9,99 € (D)

Compact Lernkrimi Sprachkurs

› Sprachen lernen für Anfänger

› Krimigeschichte in 10 Lektionen

› Vokabelkarten zum kostenlosen Download

14,99 € (D)

Compact Lernkrimi Rätselblock

› 10 Mini-Krimis mit 90 Rätselübungen

› Lösungen und Vokabelangaben auf der Rückseite

› Zahlreiche Illustrationen

5,99 € (D)

›› Jeder Band inklusive Abschlusstest und Glossar

Englisch | Spanisch | Italienisch | Französisch | DaF | Schwedisch

www.lernkrimi.de
www.compactverlag.de